The Minotaur at Calle Lanza
Zito Madu

T0051641

Printed in the United States of America
First edition 2024
1 2 3 4 5 6 7 8 9

ISBN: 978-1-953368-66-9

Belt Publishing
13443 Detroit Avenue, Lakewood, OH 44107
www.beltpublishing.com

Cover art by David Wilson
Book design by David Wilson

1

Venice is one of those extraordinarily strange places in the world. Before I landed there in the fall of 2020, it had been made known to me so much through literature, photos, paintings, and stories told by friends and friends of friends. But instead of all that information making it real and graspable, it rather made it seem so fantastical that on the very first day I walked around the city, I stopped once, pushed my feet hard on the cobblestone streets and, feeling their concreteness, told myself, yes, this is a place that's as real as everywhere else.

My flight from Amsterdam to Venice was short. Though there had been more people on the plane than the one I'd taken from Detroit to Amsterdam, it was still relatively empty. When we landed, I was surprised at how small Marco Polo Airport was. It was a standard airport, but standard was good for me. It was easy to get my lone bag and find my way outside. In the open, I realized my phone had no signal—it couldn't even connect to the airport's Wi-Fi. To make matters worse, I didn't speak any Italian, which meant asking for help was going to be difficult. I somehow managed to retain none of the language I'd picked up from years of watching and reading about AC Milan and following Serie A. Looking around, I didn't see anyone who seemed like a worker or an authority figure, and so, not knowing what to do, not knowing how to get from Marco Polo to the apartment I was supposed to be staying at in the city, I sat on top of my bag in front of the airport and waited.

I was waiting. Waiting for the time to pass. Waiting because I was tired and because being in Venice, especially on my first visit, felt strange at the time. I was waiting for something to happen. Nothing in particular but something. If I had been more religious, I would say I was waiting for a sign. But I wasn't, and I'm not religious. It also wasn't quite right to say I was just waiting. That's only one part of it. The other part is that I was sitting there, being held in place by the guilt of leaving my parents behind when they needed me the most. They were perfectly within the demographic of older people who were deemed highly vulnerable at the time, and being teachers who were pushed into remote instruction, they were struggling with their day-to-day work while trying to survive from the larger catastrophe.

While stuck, I thought about how small Marco Polo Airport was. Its smallness made it feel more welcoming and less intimidating than I had expected. I felt like I had landed in a small town, not a city like Paris, London, or New York. Understandably, because international—and local—travel was heavily restricted, there weren't too many people around. A few walked in and out of the airport as

I sat there. Some glanced at me in passing. Others looked longer. I pretended not to see them.

2

The first place I ever saw outside of Nigeria was Paris—from the inside of Charles de Gaulle Airport. I was seven at the time. The sight left a deep impression on me. It didn't make me want to go back to Paris in particular, but for a young child who had only been in his village and the villages around it before, that first glimpse of Paris blasted my mind open to the fact that there was so much to see in the world. I still feel attached to that airport, which for me was the sight of a second birth.

Before that, I lived with my family in a village in Imo State in southeastern Nigeria. Our great adventure out of that small part of the world began because of a tease and a test of friendship. Years before our flight out to Paris, my then pregnant mother was walking with a friend to the traditional August meeting for Igbo women. The friend was walking quickly ahead of my mother because she was trying to drop off visa lottery applications for her family before the meeting started. My mother was exhausted, and she joked to her friend that their friendship must not be close because the friend hadn't gotten applications for our family. For my mother, it was an inconsequential quip, but the next day, the woman showed up with several applications to prove her friendship. My mother filled the papers out and sent them off. Time went on and she forgot about them.

A while after that, she received a response that said the applications had been approved and that our family had been accepted to go through the rest of the process. This meant more papers to fill out, as well as interviews and expensive payments. My father, knowing that there were many scams around the immigration process, and grifters taking advantage of people's desperation to leave, judged the letters of approval to be fake. He put the paperwork away and forgot about it until one of his friends from the States came over to see him the night before his flight. As is tradition with my father and his friends, the two of them stayed up through the night, drinking and trading stories. In the early hours of the morning, my father's friend brought up the idea of our family possibly immigrating, which my father dismissed, noting that he had already received scam approval papers. His friend, curious about the letters, asked if he could see them. My father showed him, but rather than the friend laughing along with the joke, he said that the papers were, in fact, real. My father needed to fill out the documents immediately; the friend would take them to the embassy on his way back to the States. In the morning's early hours, my parents, suddenly filled with the possibility of a new life elsewhere, completed the rest of the paperwork, helped by Wite-Out, and sent it off.

What followed was a long process of receiving more papers, filling them out, traveling from the village to Port

Harcourt and Lagos to fill out even more papers, and going through multiple interviews—all with the stress of possibly uprooting our family and moving to the US. The process cost my father almost everything financially. At the time, there were seven of us, though my mother was pregnant. All the land my father's father had left for him and his siblings he sold to fund the migration process—a personal shame and failure he still carries with him. Even worse, when the application costs exceeded all the money we had, my father, who has all the pride in the world, went and, as he puts it, begged people for help. He still carries this shame with him as well.

By luck and grace, we managed to get visas for my entire family, an unprecedented result in the immigration lottery. Usually, visas were given out to only a few family members. According to my mother, the first day my father went to pick up our visas, he was given four. When he returned the second morning to pick up the last three, he was refused by the woman working the counter. She said that they hadn't given out more than four for one family before. My father begged the woman, but she refused. This was happening on the second floor of the building, and not knowing what to do, seeing that the woman would not budge, he headed toward the stairs. That's when he ran into the consulate officer who had given him the first four visas, and she asked him if he had picked up the remaining ones. He said no, and instead of reporting that he had been refused, he simply said that he was only just getting there to pick up the rest. The officer then took him back upstairs, where he waited by the counter as she went behind to pick up the rest of the visas and hand them to him. He paid for the rest and left. Our plan was then that four of us would go first—my father and the three oldest children: my older brother, my younger sister, and me. We were to establish ourselves there before my pregnant mother and my other sister and brother would join us. More than anything, it was a financial matter; the others had to wait until my father could find enough money to pay for their combined flights.

I remember the cold of September 1998 in Detroit, Michigan. I remember the thrill of seeing a yellow light. I remember moving to the small room on the second floor of the house on Clements Street on the city's West Side. Our landlord, Mr. Collins, had a handlebar mustache and wore a cowboy hat and cowboy boots. I had never seen anyone like that before. Since we had no winter clothes when we arrived, Mr. Collins and his wife, Cookie, gave us the coats and sweaters their adult children had worn when they were younger. Mr. Collins gave my father a long Oakland Raiders coat that had belonged to him. My favorite picture of my father is of him standing in the snow with that coat on, sporting the buzzcut that he would shave off a few years later, going bald in order to save the ten-dollar cost of a haircut and instead spend it on his children.

My youngest brother was born in the States at the end of that October, soon after my mother and the others arrived. All eight of us lived in a small room in that house. In those days, my father worked as a stock boy at Rite Aid. He had to do this after he and my mother learned that all their teaching certifications and years of work in Nigeria meant nothing in the States. Turning a corner in the maze of memory, I see the eight of us huddled around a space heater in that one room. I can still feel the cold of that first winter.

As time passed and my mother and father found more footing, we were able to rent the whole top floor of the house. Later on, we moved to the bottom floor, which was bigger, while Mr. Collins's son, whose face I remember but whose name I can't, lived upstairs with his on-and-off girlfriend. The son was addicted to drugs at the time, and to stay on his good side, my father would give him money whenever he asked. Once, my father refused, and in the middle of the street, Mr. Collins's son attacked him, punching and kicking him while my father refused to fight back. My brothers and sisters and I watched this scene with our mother through the screen door of our house. Afterward, and throughout my childhood, I was angry at my father for letting himself be so humiliated. I couldn't imagine letting myself be dominated as he had, and it felt so humiliating to watch a man who I knew was powerful, physically and in terms of his personality, be beaten up in the middle of the street. I would have fought back, but my father didn't, and I was angry at him for his restraint, which seemed like cowardice and fear at the time. For a long time I didn't forgive him for it. But my anger was a childish anger. The kind of anger that is possible because I didn't understand the world at that age. I was a child who felt like he had nothing to lose. When I brought the incident up with my father as an adult, he was surprised that I remembered and still cared about it. Explaining himself, he said he couldn't have taken the chance of fighting back for two reasons. He didn't want to hurt the man because he was Mr. Collins's son, and Mr. Collins had been kind to us. And he didn't want to fight back for fear that if the other man had a weapon and my father was killed, there would be no one to take care of us. Suffering a small humiliation under those circumstances was worthwhile. It was necessary. Soon after the fight, Mr. Collins's son and his girlfriend moved out, and we lived in the house alone.

By then, I was already getting into trouble everywhere but especially at school. My first fight happened on the playground at Macculloch Elementary. From the beginning, kids made fun of my accent and clothes, but I didn't care too much about that. It has always taken much more than insults to touch me. What touched me was being at recess, under a strange metal dome the kids would play under, and a kid who had been auditioning to be my bully for some time challenged me to a first-blood match. The first-blood match came from World Wrestling Entertainment (then the World Wrestling Federation), and the rules of the fight were simple: whoever bled first lost.

The fight had hardly begun before he grabbed my head and slammed it against the side of the metal dome. Blood gushed from my nose. I tried to argue that he hadn't won because I got nosebleeds all the time, an inheritance from my father and grandfather. The other kids laughed, and the wannabe bully celebrated his victory. I was in such pain and filled with so much rage. Each drop of blood only made me angrier. As he was celebrating, I launched myself at him, and we fought until teachers separated us. We were taken to the principal's office, and my father was called to the school. I was told to apologize but I refused. I had done nothing wrong, and I was still angry that I hadn't hurt the kid even more. Thinking about it today, I still wish I would have slammed his head against the metal to let him feel the same pain I did.

A few more kids tried to play the role of my bully, and each attempt led to a fight. Those young days established a pattern between my father and me: I got in trouble, he was alerted, and then he punished me in the car and at home. First it was yelling, then it was hitting, and then the hits got harder and harder. Until I went to college, this was the main structure of our relationship.

Within that structure were still moments that reminded me of the relationship my father and I had before we moved to the States. Times when I looked at him as if he was the greatest man in the world. Once, he was called to my elementary school because a teacher claimed I had stolen a book from her class. I hadn't. When he came into the class and pulled me up from my seat, I had my head down. Considering that stealing was one of the worst acts one could commit in our family, the accusation alone was a terrible shame, and I was dreading the punishment. After my father came and listened to the teacher, he asked me in Igbo if I had taken the book. I will never forget the intensity in his eyes. I told him I hadn't. He asked me to be honest with him. I told him that I hadn't stolen the book. He then took me by his side and told the teacher she was wrong. He told her our family didn't steal and warned her to never accuse me of stealing and to not waste his time again.

Seeing Paris in the distance through the windows of Charles de Gaulle Airport when I was young planted the seed, but what fertilized the need to leave our home in Detroit was the feeling that I couldn't survive there with my father. I never felt that I was alive in the same house as him. I couldn't be anything but angry, and I was angry all of the time. Angry at him and at the horrible luck to be born to him, to have been someone like myself, where my existence was a crime I was punished for every day. After so many years of almost daily punishments, I realized the problem was simple, and the simplicity made any real solution impossible. I was the problem. Not particularly anything that I was doing. It was me as a person. Those two reasons—to see the world and to live—pushed me to leave our house whenever I had the chance, whether that was playing soccer—sometimes staying at my coach's house until I had no choice but to go home—or taking a ten-hour Greyhound bus alone to see New York City. Each time I was able to leave helped me plot what I saw as my ultimate fight for freedom, the call for adventure that would mean I would leave that house on Clements Street and never return again. Many times when we fought, I would tell my father directly that he was only going to be able to get away with it for so long. When I could finally leave, I would leave forever. My escape would be final. I dreamed of it while being trapped with a father who hated me, and with siblings who had been taught to distance themselves from me. I was going to leave, and he and everyone else in the family would never see me again.

Each time I was punished—yelled at, hit with a hand, a shoe, a belt, or whatever object was close—I welcomed it. I knew that one day, I would escape and never see any of them again. I had seen Paris and was sure to see it again. On my own, as master of my own life. To steel myself while waiting for my new life in those years, I went deep into myself, so far into the labyrinth that no one could find me. Not my father, not anyone else.

I left our house and Detroit whenever I could afford to. In my first year of college at University of Detroit Mercy, I lived in the dorms, which were about ten minutes from the second house we moved into. I could have saved money by commuting, but there was no choice for me. When I was kicked out of that college—my disinterest in school hadn't changed—I went to Wayne State University, which was twenty minutes away. I stayed in the dorms there as well. Soon the grades and the withdrawals that resulted from my poor attendance led to the scholarship money drying up. Soon I found myself back home. I didn't care about failing my classes, but because of that smaller failure, I had failed myself.

Thankfully, I had a car at the time. In Detroit, having a car is how one comes into being—an extreme version of the grand American story. Through my car, I existed. I could experience the world around me and leave home whenever I wanted. I drove everywhere all the time. I stayed out until late at night, and sometimes I sat in the car in parking lots alone rather than go back to our house. When I got home,

I would often sit in the driveway for hours, waiting for the last moment possible to go inside. Sometimes my father took away my keys as punishment, so I would take the bus and taxis to get around. I had friends pick me up, and a few times, I walked wherever I had to go. Walking always scared my mother, considering how dangerous Detroit was at that time, but that risk was worth it to the young me.

My mother sometimes teases me now that the escape I wanted so badly, that I dreamed about and suffered for, never came. She jokes that the child who wanted to leave the most is the one who ended up staying behind. Part of why I never left was because being such a black sheep put me at a disadvantage in the world outside of college. I won't condemn myself for how much of the college experience I wasted, because back then, I was so angry I was being forced to go through that path, which I had such a deep disdain for that I couldn't force myself to simply do the bare minimum to get through it. In those years, I was saying no by refusing to go through the performance of it all. But there is some shame now in knowing that if I could have simply done a bit more, then I could have had the freedom I wanted earlier.

When I left school, there was nothing I wanted to do. I worked at an engineering company, then traveled to Turkey to play soccer, but after each adventure, I found myself back home. It was my start and end point, my home base, and the routine was set: I went out, explored the world and myself, and then returned home.

I was slow to accept it, but what kept me at home was devotion. For my siblings, my position of responsibility was clear. After my older brother left for college, my other brothers and sisters needed someone who could take care of them as they made their way through middle school and high school and then went on to college and the world after that. With my parents working until late at night, that responsibility fell to me. I became the surrogate father. I took them to school, picked them up, took them to after-school events, and then brought them home. More and more, my own life was pushed to the margins in service of theirs. Even when I was living in the dorms at the two different universities, I was still responsible for them because I was close to home.

I resented this responsibility, though I never gave it up. The option to say no was never a real one. I entertained it. I told myself that it would be easy to stop. After all, none of my siblings had stepped in to save me through the years. No one stood in front of the belt for me. I owed them nothing. Yet I never could say no to this responsibility. So I complained endlessly. I saw time and my life passing in favor of theirs. I saw them moving through the world with my help, realizing who they were and chasing their dreams elsewhere while I stood back.

The day before my youngest brother was to go off to college, I got a phone call from my mother. I was in New York City at the time. She told me he wanted me to take him to school and was refusing for anyone else to do so. I said to her that taking him was impossible—I wasn't his parent, and driving him to college wasn't my responsibility. More than that, though, they were asking me to cut my time in New York short, to give up my own life in service of his. I was angry, but she kept asking and saying that it was what he wanted.

A few hundred dollars later, and after a very early flight, I was back home. The next morning, I drove my brother almost three hours to Michigan State University and helped him set up his first dorm room. Before driving back, I lingered, taking him to lunch, and I found myself having to fight back a sudden sadness that had taken me by surprise, a sadness that came from realizing my youngest brother, who I had practically raised from the time he was in elementary school, was becoming an adult. When we hugged goodbye, I stood around not knowing what else to say or give him at that point.

That night, my mother and I sat on our porch, talking. I was still frustrated about having to fly in to take my youngest brother to school, and I said to her openly that I had been forced to sacrifice my life for her other children. It wasn't fair. I'd never asked for it, and now the youngest was going to college, and I felt I still hadn't started my own life. It was getting too late for me. She acknowledged that, and then she said there were some people who were put in the world to be helpers, that it was a gift that so many people depended on me. But what I felt at the time was that years of my life had been wasted for other people. It felt to me like an extension of the punishment I had dealt with when I was younger. Rather than being dismissed completely as the black sheep who wasn't worthwhile, that worthlessness had been transformed into service for everyone else.

When all my brothers and sisters left home, I had the chance to leave as well. But I didn't. After I had gone everywhere—from Chicago to London and back to Paris, over and over again—I still returned home and stayed. I never fully left. I still dreamed of escaping, still told myself that I was just waiting for the right time, the best conditions, for one more thing to work out before I could leave. Eventually, I reasoned that what held me back was the fact that my parents needed me. They were getting old. And I was the one who had been with them the whole time, the one who helped them with technology, who could drive them long distances, who had the kind of remote job that allowed me to be close to them. As I'd done with my siblings, I told myself I could not abandon them, and because I had to convince myself that my staying wasn't a choice, I secretly resented them.

That was only a small consolation I was granting myself, though. The truth wasn't as soothing. The reason I needed the story of being held back was that if I remained trapped, it meant I was still faithful to the dreams of my younger self. I told myself I couldn't abandon my siblings or my parents, that I was being forced to give up my life for theirs. This was true in part but not completely honest. I was also staying because I was devoted to them by choice, even if they, and my father especially, hadn't been devoted to me. I loved them, and I loved him, and this was embarrassing. To love and not be loved in return. To be dismissed and punished for most of my young life and then to find myself still at his feet.

I was in London when the pandemic began. I had gone there to celebrate my birthday in January, and as I had done many times before, I stayed over for the next two months. That March, a friend and I were planning to go to Tokyo; it was to be my first time there. Yet as the news of the virus kept getting worse, and as the seriousness of the situation settled in, I realized there was only one place for me to be. My mother and father had developed ailments and high blood pressure from all the stress of their adventure in the United States. With the virus especially threatening older people with preexisting conditions, I knew I had to go home to shield them from it as much as possible.

I went home March 10, and from then until November, I did everything for them. I helped them transition from in-person to online teaching. I tried to teach them as much as I understood about the new systems the schools told them to use, and I showed them how to use Microsoft Teams, the world's worst application. I shopped for them. I took them to large parks to exercise. I interpreted the news that was coming faster from social media than it was from cable news.

Then, that November, I was offered a residency in Venice. The CEO of Venezia FC, a soccer team in Serie B, had started an artists' residency as part of his efforts to turn the team into a global entity of fashion, culture, and sports. I was invited along with a few other artists.

There were many reasons to worry, including the overall situation of the world, but I was particularly worried about the length of the residency, which was supposed to be for six months or longer. I couldn't commit to that much time. Being away that long from people who needed me was the kind of abandonment I wasn't capable of, and I first wanted to turn down the residency. It was my father who said such an opportunity didn't come twice. He said I had already done enough for them and that it wouldn't be fair for me to lose out on the residency for their sake. I agreed to only do one month away and told them I would continue helping them with their work by remoting into their computers and by ordering food deliveries so they didn't need to leave the house. None of us were truly happy with that compromise. The day I was to leave, my father hugged me, which is always a strange event, and then, not wanting me to see his eyes tear up, he went to lay down in his room. It was only my mother who stood by the door and waved goodbye.

My flight went from Detroit to Amsterdam, where we had a layover for a few hours. At the Amsterdam airport, passengers were tested for COVID, and those without proper masks were given the right ones before being sent to passport control. The two short lines in the non-EU area were as much of a spooky consequence of the time as anything else. The whole space was unusually quiet, and all of us nervously trudged toward the two officers ahead, exchanging glances each time space opened up in front of us. The two officers were sitting in high booths, enclosed in glass, making it seem as if we were walking toward a kind of judgment, which, in essence, is what passing through passport control is. At first, I thought the two officers were like two saints at the gates of heaven who would let us into paradise according to our worthiness. But as I got closer to them, I instead saw them as something else. It seemed blasphemous to imagine saints as border officers, and with the way the officers looked at people coming through without regarding them, I thought of them as Minos and Rhadamanthus, the judges in the underworld. This comparison was unfair to the former kings, but the tension of the situation, and the way we were moving toward them like shades of human beings, matched more with their realm than that of the Christian heaven.

I was discussing with myself about whether it was fair to compare the officers to Minos and Rhadamanthus when my concentration was broken by the voice of a West African man at the front of the line. He was arguing with Rhadamanthus, and Rhadamanthus was telling the man he would not be allowed to go any further. The man, who was trying to maintain his composure, explained to the officer over and over, changing the order of his argument each time, that he had just left to go back home to Cameroon for a week and was coming back to finish his work. He had all the papers to prove it. He refashioned his argument several times, and Rhadamanthus said no to each one. No. That was it. He told the man he would not be allowed to go any further and to move to the side so that he could attend to the other passengers. The man, bubbling with frustration and anger, obeyed and waited for his chance to try his argument once more.

As I was watching him, I felt a tap on my shoulder, a strange sensation in a time when people were directed not to even stand close to each other. The person behind me was telling me that Minos was calling me forward. I walked up, holding my passport in one hand and the letter stating I was traveling for business in the other. I had rehearsed all my answers to the officer's potential questions. I could state what I was there for and give the exact address where I was staying. I could expand on the idea of my profession enough that it would be so vague as to sound important, but I also knew that giving more information than necessary would be suspicious. So I decided to only answer what Minos asked and to give the letter only if he demanded evidence of the trip's nature. When I handed him my passport, he flipped through it and asked me the standard questions. How long I would be there, what I was there for, where I was staying. I answered as directly as possible. Without looking at me, he stamped the passport, handed it back, and called the next person forward.

I took my passport and walked beyond the border separating the chosen from the soon-to-be judged. The border that also separated me from the Cameroonian man who was still waiting. I looked back at him, not knowing what to do. We were separated by two officers and an imaginary line but also by our different passports and simple chance. It was pure chance my family had won the immigration lottery in the late nineties. And if I had been using my Nigerian passport instead of my American one, it was very possible I would have been in the same situation he was. I wanted to be able to do something for him, but that thought was only to flatter myself in the moment. It was pure sentimentality. There was nothing I could do for him as we were. Challenging the judges would only get me sent to the side without allowing him to move forward. This wouldn't have helped. What he needed was fairness from the system, in the sense that he needed to be heard, understood, and granted permission to continue his journey. As I looked back, he turned and looked at me. He must have felt my attention. Our eyes met, and then I looked down to avoid his gaze. I turned around and walked away, further ahead in shame, toward my connecting flight.

3

Outside the Venice airport, I thought about my parents back in Detroit. They're both teachers who help children with learning disabilities transition to general classrooms. Like many educators during the pandemic, they were suddenly forced to teach online. It was a difficult transition. They've both taught for over thirty years, in Nigeria and the United States, but almost always in person. Like many immigrant parents, or generally older people, they struggle a lot with technology. The pandemic meant that their jobs suddenly depended on them not only using a computer full-time but also learning new processes and programs with little time for acclimation. They also had to communicate these processes and programs to their students, who often had to be supervised by parents, who, at the time, because of the general poverty of the city of Detroit and particularly its Black residents, were considered essential workers and so were often not at home. When those parents were present in the classes, they were understandably exhausted and so were very irritable. Many of them also struggled with technology and the new programs and processes as much as my parents did.

I knew this because, as I've done since my family first came to the States, I was the chief technology expert for my parents. My other five siblings would substitute when I wasn't available due to work, exercise, or when I purposely ignored their calls because I was tired of fixing their problems.

When the pandemic started, as soon as my parents were ordered to work online, I spent most days paying half-attention to my work and meetings and running downstairs every few minutes when my parents texted or called me to help them figure out something or, worse, to diagnose and fix a problem with Microsoft Teams. Issues seemed to arise every single day. Sometimes, I would bring my laptop downstairs and work from the living room. It would be me in that room, my mother in the dining room on our family desktop, and my father in my sister's bedroom at the back of the house on his school-issued laptop. The two of them in their classes and me in endless meetings. Day after day passed like this, days of frustrations. Most problems were fixable, but sometimes the problems would lead to arguments and tears. Still, I was grateful for that time with them, that there was still time with them. Opposite our house, there was a care home. Between our moments of frustration, and sometimes during a lull in our schedule, we would often see an ambulance come to pick up someone who had died there.

The time spent helping my parents out at home reminded us of the nights when I was in high school, when they would take me to their classes as they were completing their master's degrees. After arriving in the States, they discovered all of their professional certifications were invalid, and they realized they had to go to school to become teachers again. For years, they worked odd jobs; besides working at Rite Aid, my father also sold wine around the city. They were both substitute teachers, then full-time teachers, and then special education teachers. They brought me along to those classes because the teacher spoke too fast for them, and they were struggling with the work that needed to be done on the computer.

It should have been my older brother who assumed this responsibility, but a few things were working against me. I had spent more time with computers—from taking classes at school to building my own from the pieces I was allowed to take home—than anyone else in my family. My other siblings were too young. My older brother was also, admittedly, the more responsible one; he could watch the younger ones, whereas I would have been focused on other things. Looking back, this makes my parents' decision to have me help them ironic; I had to help because I was the black sheep of the family. I was the troublemaker, the rogue as my father once put it, or, as he also said many times, the failure.

In those days, my parents often received calls about my behavior at school—insubordination, fighting, and lack of effort—and then after we all came home, I would get in the car with them and drive to Wayne State University for their classes. Both of them, but mostly my father, would yell at me for the endless things I had done wrong. Then I would sit in those classes with them, take notes, ask questions, and guide them through the process of submitting work online. On the nights they didn't have class, I would help them do research and type up their papers at home, sometimes before or after being hit and yelled at for some misbehavior. Because my father is a very educated man, he used turns of phrase and words that were unfamiliar to me. He also writes in small print, and I often had to ask him to clarify some words or lines when I was typing out the papers he had written freehand. Having to ask him to tell me whether a letter was a "b" or an "f" was terrifying. If I could type out the paper without ever speaking to him, then I could have some peace. But the second I ran into an issue, my heart would drop. Most times he wouldn't be angry; it would only be a simple clarification. But sometimes he would get so upset, as if the fault was with me, that I would then type out the rest without consulting him.

At the time, I had so much anger, so much animosity, toward him. It was much less than he had for me but enough to often overwhelm my younger self. That rage with all of its tears seemed to flare up every moment the two of us were together. And the more it happened, the more I learned that it made me more vulnerable. I felt like I was being extinguished by him. To avoid this, when I typed his papers,

I often tried to use context clues or guess at a word or phrase. This often led to him becoming frustrated and so angry when he read the work back and noticed the errors that it made the situation and our relationship even worse.

Those days were so long ago that I can only really remember that time and its problems as one blended big picture. I remember always, deep down, loving my father, but what I could not understand was why he hated me so much.

I was thinking of all of this outside Marco Polo Airport when, eventually, something did happen. A short balding man who had been watching me since I had first sat down came toward me, speaking Italian quickly, which I didn't understand. I wouldn't have understood if he had spoken it slowly either. Thankfully for me, the stereotype of Italians talking with their hands seemed to be true, and I could see he was pointing me toward one of the buses lined up behind him. I grabbed my suitcase and he grabbed my left hand to guide me. At the front of the bus, I handed him a twenty-euro note. As I took another step, he grabbed my hand again, holding me back gently in order to give me change. I shook my head and then got on the bus. As we pulled away, he stood by the side watching, and he waved at me.

On the bus, I figured out a temporary fix for my phone's lack of connection. Whenever the bus stopped, I tried to connect to the public Wi-Fi of the surrounding hotels and restaurants. Then, in short bursts, I would message my friends, family, and Ted, the man who was responsible for me being in Venice. He assured me the bus was heading to the Piazzale Roma, the main bus terminal and entrance to the island. There, I could get a SIM card as a real solution to my phone issues. Then, since cars and bicycles were prohibited on the island, I could navigate on foot to the apartment that was rented for me.

There was something magical about traveling across the Ponte della Libertà. Where the airport and the mainland—where people arrived and got on and off buses just like anywhere else in the world—was satisfying in its normality, the bridge to the historical city had the feel of an adventure. It's long with what, for a few minutes, feels like endless water on both sides. A seagull followed our bus for a short while before perching on one of the poles that jutted out over the water, as if had been sent to watch and guide us forward. Even in my exhausted state, the closer we got to the terminal, the more excited I got. The drive was like a grand gesture signaling that we were going somewhere unique, a place out of the ordinary. It reminded me of my first visit to Marseille, the wonder of seeing the city and its water after our train emerged from a long tunnel.

The first thing I saw at the entrance of Piazzale Roma were a group of uniformed men standing on the left side, talking and laughing among themselves. They looked like police but were armed like military. The sight of them sapped my excitement. When I stepped off the bus and grabbed my bag, I went to the far right and stood behind the cabs that were lined up there, out of sight of the heavily armed men. Though I had a reason to be there and all the valid papers, I could also see with a quick glance that I was one of the few Black people around. The last thing I wanted was to engage them.

After a few minutes of trying to change the settings on my phone to make it work, I made my way to a small store—it was more of a stand than a store—under the Ponte della Costituzione. The lady there told me she didn't sell SIM cards but that there was a mart nearby that did. She pointed behind me and said it was next to the Bar Ristorante Autorimessa. I could see that it was next to the carabinieri office, which explained the group of armed men a small distance away.

There were two crosswalks to pass before getting to the store. I stood in front of the first one for a few minutes with people walking around me, going to and coming from across the bridge behind me. I kept looking at the armed men, hoping that something would compel them to leave. I had done nothing to them and they had done nothing to me, but I knew police were police everywhere. Innocence is a delicate concept, especially when it comes up between a regular person—and a Black foreign tourist at that—and an agent of the state. Through all of my engagements with police officers in the United States, Nigeria, the United Kingdom, France, and other countries, I knew the most important thing was to avoid contact with them. Out of both fear and practicality. No matter how right I was, or how valid my stay in Venice was, I didn't want to be in the position of having to answer any questions about it. I considered trying my luck at finding the apartment without directions rather than crossing the street but that seemed a path to more trouble.

Eventually, I crossed. And then I went through the second crosswalk on the right along with a number of other people. I went into the store and bought a SIM card, and the woman there helped me put twenty euros on the card and gave me a small pin to open the compartment on my phone.

My next goal was to find my way to the apartment. As I learned later, I could have just taken one of the water buses from the Piazzale Roma and gone to the Salute stop at Dorsoduro in less than thirty minutes. Instead, I dragged my bag along while looking at the directions on my phone, which still had an unstable signal. The walk was also supposed to take less than thirty minutes, but there were so many times when I was exasperated by the street names changing and becoming different without any supposed rhyme or reason—Fondamenta Pigan to Fondamenta Cazziola—the road splitting into different paths that ran close to each other but led to very different areas, and, my favorite frustration, the times I would turn down a road, expecting it to continue, and only find it ran into the water or a dead end. I walked into so many dead ends I started playing a personal guessing game, predicting whether each new turn would lead me somewhere worthwhile or into another cul-de-sac. When I reached the Gallerie dell'Accademia, I felt triumphant. I had made it through most of the labyrinth. At least in the area that I was in. I sat down on my bag again, this time to relax, recover, and savor my achievement. I watched a couple of girls take selfies in front of the door to the gallery, which was closed like so many other places around.

After about ten minutes, I continued the journey. The rest of the walk was fairly straightforward, though not less mythical. The small streets surrounded by tall walls on both sides felt like alleys, and they made me feel again like I had felt in the bus on the bridge, as if I were entering a secret world. Each time I turned, what came after was a delightful surprise. The design of the island made the ordinary delightful. Going over the stairs at Calle de la Chiesa and through Fondamenta Venier dai Leon, only to come out and see an ice cream shop on the left, made me so happy that I almost stopped to reward myself. A simple joy, that of childlike discovery. But hearing everyone inside speaking Italian, and also seeing that I would again be the only Black person there, put me off for the moment, and I continued on without the reward.

I walked past the Peggy Guggenheim Collection, which was closed, but what caught my attention at that turn was a small bronze statue in the window of the opposite gallery. I believe it was called the Ravagnan Gallery. It was a statue of a businessman with a suitcase, but half of his body was missing—half of the torso on the right, and then the lower part of the body on the left, which made it seem as if the statue was floating in air. I looked around for some information about it in the window but there was nothing. Only the half-businessman facing the world outside.

My apartment building was less than three minutes from the gallery. When I turned right on Calle Lanza, which had the typical high walls but strangely more space than the other streets in the labyrinth, there was a blond man sitting outside waiting for me. We introduced ourselves. He was the owner of the apartment, which he had inherited from his family, though he spent most of his time in Rome. He took my bag up the first set of stairs and opened the only door of that floor to the left.

The apartment was cozy. There was a bathroom to the right and a small area to the left, which served as a living room, kitchen, and dining room—a small table with two chairs. In the living room, a gray couch faced a small, mounted television, and on the counter next to the television was the stove, the sink, and an electric kettle with a number of different teas and coffee bags next to it. Down the hallway was a locked door, which he told me was a second bedroom—his bedroom—and to the left of it was the one I would be sleeping in, with two beds pushed together to form one bigger one with small pillows stuffed in the divide.

On the side table next to the couch, he set down a map of Venice. Using a red marker, he circled everywhere he thought would be useful to me: grocery stores, restaurants, churches that were open to the public, and then the parts of San Marco tourists often loved to explore. We were in Dorsoduro, a more reserved and quieter area, made even quieter by the lack of visitors and the businesses that were shut down at the time. When he was done, he folded up the map and gave it to me. We said our goodbyes and, in a risky move, shook hands before he departed.

It was either two or three in the afternoon when he left. I was exhausted and hungry but more exhausted than hungry. I undressed and went to sleep. When I woke up, it was past seven in the evening. Tiredness was still there, but the hunger had taken precedent. Still a bit dazed, and forgetting the map I'd been given a few hours before, I went searching for food. My plan was simply to retrace my steps toward the Piazzale Roma, hoping to run into a restaurant or a store along the way.

The lack of absurdly bright streetlights made it much darker than I was used to in the cities in the States. But there was something else that was strange to me. I took a few steps until I stood as still as a bronze statue, trying to pinpoint it. Walking can be conducive to thought, but for me, what is essential is stillness. My thoughts flutter around like butterflies, and I need to be still as they exhaust themselves before returning home. This time, it didn't take long, and the phenomenon I was trying to name was part of the reason.

Venice was quiet. There was the lack of foot traffic, but what seemed so strange to me, because it was such a normal part of my hearing life elsewhere, was the lack of car noise. There were no sounds of honking horns, no tires on the road, no car doors opening or closing. It's not the first time I've had the experience of being in a place without those noises. I was born, grew up in, and still frequently visit our village in Nigeria. And there are plenty of escapes from the city sounds in the States for anyone who has the time and transportation. But it felt strange and exciting to be in the middle of a city and have it be so quiet. I could hear. Very clearly. I could hear the light footsteps and bits of conversation of the few others who were still out in the neighborhood. Laughter bounced off the walls in the darkness. I could hear the sound of running water and boats moving through those waters, even when I couldn't see them. There were rumors about dolphins returning to the waters of Venice. Rumors that were untrue and easily debunked, but as clear and clean as the environment and the water was during my time there, what I was roused to do every day was to sit around and listen to the sounds of the island that I was on.

Buoyed by the joy of small sounds, I walked down Fondamenta Venier dai Leon. Right before the open space ended and the road funneled into a narrow pathway with tall buildings on both sides, when the view of the water to the left is shut off by a wall—which felt to me the perfect structure for a road in a labyrinth—I received a text from Ted, telling me that the city was under a kind of curfew. Most restaurants closed around six or seven. An obvious sign was the fact that there were barely any people out in the dark. A few were sitting at a corner pub I passed, eating ice cream and drinking beer, but that was it. The only other person was me, standing a small distance from them in a bright yellow coat. I considered going back to the apartment to make some tea and manage for the night, but two things stopped me. The first was my hunger, which was painful. Tea could do nothing against it. The second was that I had just walked past the people at the pub and didn't want the embarrassment of walking past them again after such a short time going the other way. The quick return journey would signal to them that not only was I a person who, according to the way they had looked at me, shouldn't be there but also that I was someone who didn't know his way around.

Thankfully, I didn't have to walk far after that to find food. Right in the middle of the path, I came upon a pizza shop built into the wall. The man inside was wearing a white shirt and an apron, and he was scrolling through his phone. In front of him was a display of different slices of pizza. I recognized the cheese slices but couldn't make out the ingredients to the others. Maybe the man didn't hear me approach, or maybe he was waiting for me to make an introduction first, but when I stood in front of him, waiting for what felt like a minute, he didn't raise his head or acknowledge my presence. I stood there with a smile ready for the moment he looked at me. But he didn't. So after some time, I took a few steps forward and said, "Ciao."

The pizza man looked up and began speaking to me in Italian. I stood there smiling as if I understood him. When he stopped, I pointed at the cheese slice. Then, by his intonation, I could hear that what he said next was a question, but not knowing what the question was, I just stood there pointing at the slice of pizza. He then repeated the question and also gave me hints for an answer. Una. Due. Tre. He put up one, two, and then three fingers, again without any sign of being irritated or annoyed. I responded so emphatically that it felt like a sudden shout: "Due!" He took out two slices, heated them up, and gave them to me on a plate. Then he went back to his phone. I took a few steps back and for however long it took for me to eat the two slices of pizza, the man and I stood opposite each other in quietness. Beyond my chewing, the sounds of distant footsteps, running water, and the conversation and laughter from the pub accompanied us. The moment made me very happy.

I was so happy that after saying goodbye to the man and going home for the night, I was already looking forward to seeing him the next day. But the following morning, on my walk to the Piazzale Roma, where I went into one of the restaurants to buy a chicken sandwich, I saw that the pizza shop was closed. It was also closed when I came back that evening.

In the small area before turning onto Campiello Barbaro that evening, I saw a musician. Well, I heard his music first, and it drew me toward him. He was dressed in all black, with a round black hat, and he was playing a type of guitar I had never seen before. The open case in front of him doubled as a collection plate. The song he played felt as if it was coming out of the walls around us and at the same time from inside my body. The notes ran up against and beneath my skin. I stood there listening to him play for a few minutes. People walked past the two of us, and no one else seemed to pay him any attention. After I paid him and walked away, the absurd thought came to me that I was the only one who could see the musician in black.

I heard and saw the musician in black once more during my stay in the city. But throughout my time there, on all of my walks down and back from the pathway of Fondamenta Venier dai Leon, during the days, the evenings, and the nights, I never again saw the pizza shop open, or the man who taught me how to order two slices.

4

The second time I saw the musician in black, the same day I went to Piazzale Roma for a chicken sandwich, I also had to go to the mainland for a computer charger. When I woke up that morning, I realized I had forgotten my charger somewhere in the Amsterdam airport during the layover. Part of me entertained letting the computer die and spending the rest of my time in the old city without the distraction and demand of the laptop screen or the endless, bullshit work that waited for me, but the entertainment of the idea was all I had. I needed a new charger—for work but more importantly for my parents. Before I left Detroit, I had enabled both of their computers so I could access them remotely and watch over them through their workday and solve any problems that came up, either by walking them through the solution step-by-step or taking over control and fixing the issue directly.

What surprised me first was that for all of the stores that could be found on the island of Venice—which included every kind of boutique, beauty, jewelry, decor, and furniture store, from the typical ones that can be found in every big and popular city in the world to the particularly Venetian ones—the island had no Apple store. That was on the mainland, at the Nave de Vero shopping center. Getting there was straightforward. From Piazzale Roma, after my chicken sandwich, I only needed to take two buses to the Centro Commerciale stop, with the stop ID of 333, before getting off and walking for about three minutes.

The second surprise was that when I got to the shopping mall, it was a typical shopping mall. I felt as I had when I'd landed at the airport, that this was a place like any other place in the world. Neither for good nor bad, just that it was another place like any other place in the world. The global brands—Apple, Dyson, GameStop, Guess, JD Sports, Lego, Levi's, McDonald's—mixed with some Italian ones, but it was a shopping mall that could have been in any other city. This made sense, of course, the same way that all the typical stores on the island did—a place that lived off tourism would reflect the brands that tourists wanted. But there was still something humorous about putting the magical idea of Venice, with all of its romance, beauty, and history, next to the fact that I could sit down and eat a double cheeseburger, or go to the mainland Apple store to buy a charger, as well. Everywhere is like everywhere else. The only difference was that in all of the other Apple stores I have been in, you usually have to ask one of their workers to help you through the process of buying anything, while in the one in mainland Venice, you are able to pick out the charger you need from a stack of them and then pay for it.

I got back to the apartment in time to begin the second half of what would come to be my daily routine during my time on the island. The morning and daytime were for me to walk around, shop, and explore the little area of Venice that I would explore. At night, I would go to the apartment to do my work, keeping a window on my laptop open for one of my parents. I took most of my meetings on my phone so they wouldn't interfere in case I needed to help them. My mother was the one who usually texted or called for help— everything I have to say about Microsoft Teams is improper. But sometimes my father would ask for help. He's not too prideful to do that, and he has never been, but these days, he hesitates before doing so. He would start each phone call by apologizing for bothering me and asking me not to be upset. "I know you don't like hearing my voice," he said.

5

Igbo people believe in reincarnation within both one's immediate and extended family. Who you were before can be identified by looks, certain birthmarks, behavioral traits, manners of speaking, and so on.

When my mother and I were in Nigeria in 2019, we went to visit her younger brother. He wasn't at home when we arrived, but his daughters were there. My mother saw, I believe, his youngest daughter, picked her up, studied her face, saw something that normal eyes could not, and declared with joy that the child was her sister who had died young. The day before, we had visited my grandparents' house, and her father, who was still alive at the time, said during a conversation that all five of his children brought him so much happiness. My mother, who was sitting opposite him, corrected him immediately, telling him that he had six children.

When my uncle finally came home that day, my mother and I were sitting in the living room. My mother had the girl on her lap, playing and doting on her throughout the conversation. For the whole time we were at her brother's home, she kept the girl by her side.

My reincarnation was determined differently. My father has always called me by the Igbo words for father or dad, like *nna*, *onye nna*, and *mpa*. Or *nna m*, *mpa m*: my father. Often, he calls me by his father's name. When my mother talks about me as a baby, she sometimes mentions that when my paternal grandmother, who died not long after I was born, would ask to hold me, she would demand I be given to her husband.

Recently, I asked my mother to tell me the story of my birth again, the story of my birth that doubles as the story of my reincarnation. Out of her six children, two of us, my youngest brother and I, had dramatic entrances into the world. My brother was born a month after we arrived in the States, and when he was in the womb, it was thought he was a twin, but after my mother went to the hospital, she was alerted that he was actually drowning in her stomach. There was too much amniotic fluid. He became the only one of us to come out through a cesarean birth.

When my mother was pregnant with me, that's when she came to live in Imo State, where my father is from; she was still living in Anambra when my older brother was born. She said that whenever she went to sleep, she would dream that my paternal grandfather, who she had never met and had only seen in photos, would pull up a dining room chair by the head of her bed. He would be wearing his red chieftain hat. She would see him, but he would say nothing in the dream. And he would sit there with her for a long time. When she woke up, she of course would not see him there. But each time she went to sleep, he would appear and sit with her again.

She told my father and Auntie Scholar—the daughter of my grandfather's sister—about the dream. Auntie Scholar came to my mother a few days before my birth and told her that she had also had a dream about me. In the dream, my grandfather went to her and told her that he was the one who was coming, and his name would be Onyekachukwu.

In the womb, I was difficult. I was big, and I twisted and kicked a lot. My mother thinks this twisting was the reason my umbilical cord wrapped around my body and my neck. Because of this, the birth was difficult, and after a certain point in being pushed, I stopped coming out. The nurses kept encouraging my mother, and she kept pushing, but I wouldn't move. When the doctor came in, he chased out the nurses, pulled out a pair of scissors, and carefully cut the umbilical cord. I was born alive, and I moved around, but I didn't cry. No matter how many times they hit me, I didn't cry. They took me out of the hospital ward, cleaned me, and wrapped me up.

After I was born, everybody, including my father, mother, and Auntie Scholar, said there was no point in choosing a name since it had already come in the dream. Nobody would change it.

The next day, very early in the morning on my first day in the world, the doctor came back. Still I was not crying.

The doctor took me and my mother's flask full of hot water, went to the end of the ward where I had been washed the day before, and then poured some of the hot water on me. Then I started crying. Loud enough that everyone in the ward could hear it. The people around my mother joked that I was so big, which was why the cry was so loud. That I was already screaming with the voice of a grown man.

All this is to say that, from the beginning, I was trapped. All three of us were: me, my father, and my grandfather, who died almost two decades before I was born, who came to my mother and his sister's daughter in a dream to announce his return. But "trapped" isn't the right word. It's too negative and not exact enough for the situation. We weren't trapped. But my birth put all three of us inside a kind of labyrinth. A structure that can be a trap, a prison, but also the manifestation of our connection and relationship, a home. An escape. A place of solitude and comfort.

In 1947, Jorge Luis Borges published a story called "The House of Asterion," in which the minotaur, in first person, explains his situation as a creature and as a creature within the labyrinth. Thirty years after publishing the story, Borges gave a lecture on nightmares at the Teatro Coliseo in Buenos Aires—a lecture that is collected in the book *Seven Nights*—where he touched on the story's inspiration. The story was linked to two nightmares he had. The first was about a labyrinth, an image he said came,

> in part, from a steel engraving I saw in a French
> book when I was a child. In this engraving were
> the Seven Wonders of the World, among them
> the labyrinth of Crete. The labyrinth was a great
> amphitheater, a very high amphitheater (and
> this was apparent because it was higher than the
> cypresses and the men outside it). In this closed
> structure—ominously closed—there were cracks.
> I believed when I was a child (or I now believe I
> believed) that if one had a magnifying glass powerful
> enough, one could look through the cracks and see
> the Minotaur in the terrible center of the labyrinth.

The second nightmare was about a mirror, and in introducing this element, Borges said: "The two are not distinct, as it only takes two facing mirrors to construct a labyrinth."

A grandfather, a son who loved and took on so many of his qualities through devotion and duty, and a grandson who was the reincarnation of that grandfather, with a similar face and heart—a labyrinth of three mirrors. At any point and at every point, each one of us is in the middle with the other two facing him.

I don't know if my father ever had higher expectations

for me than he did for any of my other siblings. Those expectations likely fell on my older brother, the first son. By nature of being the firstborn, he became the one tasked with being responsible. He was the surrogate father and parent, especially after we moved to the States, where he became the one who watched us when our parents were gone. He was the one who carried out their orders, a responsibility that must have been heavy for a child who was also trying to find his own way in a new country.

My father might not have had higher expectations for me, but the fights we had, the tension between us, the hatred that it became, hurt him more deeply than if I was just his son. One particular day, after getting another call from school about my behavior and physically disciplining me at home, he sat on the edge of his bed, exhausted. He said to me that I was the biggest regret of his life. Immediately after that, he called me by his father's name and asked what he had done to deserve such a son as a punishment. He did not look at me.

6

Years ago, before the pandemic, my family went home to our village in Nigeria. I was with my two youngest brothers, my father, and my mother. One day, my youngest brother, one of my aunts, and I were on one of the terraces to our house. They were standing, and I was laying on the ground. My aunt was chiding me for not taking time to visit the other villages and the closer cities, like I had when I was young, and like my older brother did whenever he was at home. She shook her head, laughed, and said she couldn't believe the same child who wouldn't be contained at home had turned into a man who did nothing but lay on the ground and walk around the village. My little brother added on, saying that I was even worse in our house in the States, where most of the time, I stayed in my room either reading or writing.

It's true that when I was young, I wanted nothing more than to explore the world, the world around me, and the world beyond my borders. That was happiness. That was my freedom. To be outside, running around, dancing in festivals, playing with my brother and our cousins, going to other villages to dance and play, staying out for so long it would be almost pitch-black when I came home. I wasn't unlike many children, but the collection of villages afforded freedom and safety, since everyone knew everyone and everyone knew my father. I could stay out for hours and go far, knowing that I would get home safely, either on my own or with the help of someone else. If not, I held it as a truth as evident as the rain in August that my father would come find me.

One of the stories my mother likes to tell is a story about my older brother and me being lost. We had walked to the neighboring villages to dance during a festival. It was the rainy season. We spent all day out, but when night fell, we were nowhere to be found. The rain was heavy, and my father grew worried. He hopped onto one of those motorcycles that is ever-present in the country. He looked for us in our village, asking anyone he could find if they had seen us. When he was done there, he went from village to village, doing the same. He finally found us huddled next to a building on a random road, sheltering from the rain. With so many years separating me from that event, I can only imagine my relief and joy at seeing my father arrive on the motorcycle in the rain. He sat me in front of him, and my brother sat behind him holding onto his waist, and he rescued us that night. It seemed that whenever my father and I had an especially explosive fight, to the point where I could not stand to speak or see him for days, my mother would take me into her arms or sit by me, telling stories about when I and her other children were young. Once, we were sitting on the stairs in front of our house, and I told her I hated my father, hated him with everything in my soul. She told me not to say things I didn't mean, and then she told me the story of my father rescuing my older brother and me from the rain and dark. She would tell me not to hold the things he said, and the things he did to me, against him. "That's just how he is," she would tell me, "but nothing makes him happier than his children."

My hatred of my father didn't come out of nowhere. Now that I'm older and removed from that time, I can see its causes and effects very clearly. There was a break and complete change in our relationship when we moved to the United States. My father—who had bought me my first soccer ball and put in a net so I could walk around, kicking the ball over and over until the net broke, when he would then buy a new one—became the enemy who would tell me I was the biggest mistake of his life. Without the anger now, I can see what happened and what changed.

It happened gradually, and a lot of it had to do with school. From the moment I started school, I've never liked it. In any capacity. Nothing felt more oppressive than being shut away from the life I saw and could feel in my spirit was outside. I could do the work, I could pass the classes, even the more challenging ones, but I was bored. No matter the school, or how desperately I needed to pass a class, or how often the possibilities of success and a good life were dangled in front of me as motivation, my heart kept returning to the same realization: I did not want to be in school. And when I was asked what I would do instead, the answer was "anything but this." The "this" being spending most of each day watched, instructed, controlled, punished, and fashioned into something I had no interest in becoming. And what I learned about myself that has remained true through each stage of life, each transformation, is that I can't be unfaithful to myself. A trait shared by my father and grandfather.

In Nigeria, the teachers hit me on the hands with rulers for misbehaving. In Detroit, they called my parents, kicked me out of class, sent me to detention—where I would sometimes have to stand in front of the other students, holding a dictionary in each outstretched hand—made me join the after-school volleyball team when detention became ineffective, and sent me to in-school suspension. When all of those options failed, most of my high school teachers would send me to my art class when they were done with me. My art teacher welcomed me and let me sit in the back of her classroom, at any hour, drawing until it was time for the next class.

There is a picture of my older brother and me at our first graduation in Nigeria. We're in our gowns and holding diplomas. He's looking at the camera and smiling, and my face looks like that of someone who has been condemned to some great punishment.

Being the misbehaving son of two teachers was a shame, but it wasn't just because of their occupation that my hatred for school led to so many fights and a break in love. No. As an adult now, I know that I was also being cruel to my parents, and to my father especially.

My father was just entering his twenties in the mid-seventies when my grandfather died from poisoning. Then, two of my father's older siblings died as well. He was left with only an older sister and a younger brother. He became the man of his family. He assumed his father's role in the village community, an immense position with great responsibility. He gave up some of his dreams because of poverty and because he had to take care of his family, but it made him a very commanding and proud man. In order to fund our move to the United States, he sold almost all the land he had inherited from his father. He gave up his lineage and his other dreams so that his children could have a chance at a better life in the United States.

When we arrived in the States, all the people who were supposed to help us acclimate abandoned us. That's when my father also found out that his certifications, his years as a teacher in Nigeria, and his position as a respected man in the community, a chief, meant nothing in the American world. My father, who can go back to Nigeria right now and be surrounded for days by elders from all the surrounding villages, had to take a job working nights as a Rite Aid stock boy. I remember watching him leave for his shift from the window of the one room where all of us stayed, on the second floor of the Clements Street house on Detroit's West Side.

He worked other jobs. So did my mother, who, after giving birth, started working alongside him. He spent years selling wine across the city, driving and learning the roads of Detroit in a red Toyota. He and my mother worked as substitute teachers for years. Then, once they got their degrees and certifications again, they moved into permanent positions, though they were permanent in name only. I can see all the times my parents were moved to different schools, those years when they weren't given the placements they wanted or weren't placed at all. My father always took it the hardest. Not having work was one of the few things that made him cry. My mother's response was to tell him that there was no point in crying over the problem, what was done was done. What needed to be figured out was a solution.

As a child, I didn't know why he was so hurt by the news of missing out on work, why he seemed to always be angry, and why my behavior in particular was such a flashpoint in our house, but now I think I can see it.

My father was being humiliated. Having to sell his father's land, the way his Rite Aid supervisors talked down to him, the way people made fun of his accent, the way he had to ask people to help him find work, the way he lost his status and became a nobody in this country, being told that all his decades of teaching meant nothing, having to go back to school and have people he would be teaching back home treat him like he was stupid, hearing other Nigerians who had more than us talk about how little we had, the fact that we had to live, all eight of us, in one room for a long time, the poverty, not having enough money to give his children the life he wanted them to have, to take them to Cedar Point, to let them travel, to let them see the world, the fact that had to take on so much work, all the time, to the point that it wore his body down—all these humiliations piled on top of one another, and he carried them with him every day. This was his life in the States. This was the life he gave up everything at home for.

To make matters worse, the child who was supposed to be his father decided to rebel. The things the children in our family were known for in all the schools that we attended were perfect attendance, good behavior, and excellent grades. From elementary school to college, all of us were high achieving. All but one. I was the outlier, the black sheep. The one who misbehaved. The one who got into fights. The only one who got kicked out of Cass Technical High School and had to go to Northwestern instead, where I also misbehaved and fought. The only one who has been stabbed and shot at multiple times. The only one who came home late, who hung out with the wrong people, who seemed a lost cause at everything.

I was the worst thing that could have happened to my father at the time. With the stress our precarious financial situation put on him and my mother, and with the endless daily humiliations he endured, the last thing he needed was a son who could not simply go to school and make the best of the opportunity he had sacrificed everything for. My brothers and sisters, who had their own struggles, endured and pushed ahead. I stood against him and said no.

I can see now that I was two things for him: a curse and the perfect victim. There seemed to be nothing redeemable about me, so he could hit me over and over without feeling remorse. I was goading him. He yelled at my siblings when they misbehaved, but he hardly ever hit them. He saved that for me. Once, when he accused me of stealing twenty dollars out of his pants pocket when he was asleep, he made me kneel in front of all my brothers and sisters with my hands on my head, and he whipped me with a belt so hard and for so long that for weeks I could feel the welts on my back. He kept demanding I confess to stealing the money, and I kept denying it. Now I can be honest and admit that I did take it, but the monster in me wanted to deny him the truth. At the time, I thought that he knew nothing of the humiliation of being poor outside of the house.

He made my siblings and my mother watch the punishment. None of them raised a hand to stop him. But I remember my mother being unable to take it and walking away. The point of that punishment and all the others like it was obvious to me even then. He wanted to create a break between me and the rest of my siblings. If I could not be saved, he would not allow the rogue to influence his other children.

My great sin wasn't just that I did poorly in school or that I got into trouble. It was that I wanted to live my life on my terms. I still wanted guidance, but I wanted to have input, to be the driving force for my own life. He could not grant me that. With everything he had lost, he needed to make sure that I, along with my siblings, would succeed in a way that redeemed his sacrifices. He could not give me my life, and I would not give it up to him.

From around middle school to the first two years of high school, when my father yelled, punished, and then hit me, I could not wrap my mind around how the man who had loved me so much could treat me like that. I said that I never hated my father, and that's always been true. What I wanted in those early years was to be understood by the same man who bought me soccer balls, who rescued me from the rain, who called me by his father's name. The man who once loved me.

But as the punishments went on, I transformed as well. The more he punished me, the more I wanted him to. He wanted me to change, so I misbehaved even more. I gave up all effort in school. The few things about me that still made him proud—soccer, excelling in English and math class—I stopped doing. I said to myself, deep inside my soul, that he would get nothing from me. Even worse, I challenged him. He didn't know it, but I challenged him. It was a simple battle of stamina, of endurance. I knew I was willing to be nothing, to go all the way down to hell in order to gain control of my life. I was asking him how long he would let me drag him down with me, if he had the endurance to go to the devil too.

7

The first few times I walked past the Libreria Toletta, I didn't notice it. It was in the middle of my daily walk toward Piazzale Roma, but it didn't register to me. What did register immediately was Majer, the pastry shop a few minutes away. I used to stop and stand outside it on the way to my destination and then again on my way back. Everything looked delicious through the large glass that separated me from the sweets. It must have looked strange to the workers inside to see me wearing a bright yellow jacket coming by regularly to stand outside and stare at the food. Ordinarily, I would have been just another person in a sea of thousands, an anonymous shape, but without too many other people around, I often saw the same workers, some who would turn and smile at me when they noticed me outside.

I resisted going inside for two reasons. One, because I could hear they were speaking and selling to people in Italian, and though I was sure I could walk in, inform them that I didn't speak Italian, and still receive the same warm reception and service they granted everyone else, the barrier was again something I felt would make me stand out even more.

The second reason was because I know how deceptive my eyes can be. My mother is the first person who taught me to mistrust them. When I was young, I used to ask for more food

than I could eat and then leave most of it untouched. Or I
would taste food that looked delicious and push it away when
I discovered it was not, even if I had eaten the food before and
knew it was not something I liked. My mother said then that
I ate with my eyes. Things looked good, so I went after them,
but she knew, and I knew, that I didn't actually desire those
things. I just wanted to satisfy the urge to have what looked
good. I didn't necessarily need to buy and eat the pastries; the
looking was often enough to be satisfied.

Another place that registered for me was a pizza shop
down the same road. It was not Pizzeria Ultimo. There's
nothing wrong with Pizzeria Ultimo, but it was not the
pizza shop I knew around that area. I walked in the first
time because I didn't want to keep eating the same chicken
sandwiches at the Piazzale Roma, and I was hungry to the
point that trying to decide what to eat was making me angry
on top of the frustration of hunger.

When I walked into the shop, there were only two people
there: a Middle Eastern man behind a glass display toward
the end of the shop, and, on one of the stools to my left by
the door, a teenage girl—I figured it was his daughter—who
was twirling around while looking at her phone. She didn't
raise her head or acknowledge my entrance in any way. But
the man did, and he started speaking to me in Italian. When
I walked up to the counter, I tried to explain to him that I

didn't speak Italian with the few Italian words that I knew, to which he answered in fluent Italian, which made our impasse even greater. After being fed up with the painful exchange, the daughter told her father I couldn't speak Italian. They exchanged a few more words, and his face lit up when he turned to me. Finally, we introduced ourselves to each other in English. After asking for my name, and before asking where I had come from, he asked if I was Muslim. I said I wasn't, and for a split second, he looked disappointed, but then we continued talking about other things. We talked about the weirdness of the times, about the slowness of his business, about his time in Venice. He had immigrated when he was young, and his daughter was practically Venetian through and through. He was speaking to me with the openness of someone who hadn't seen a friend in a very long time. A lull in the conversation reminded him that I had come to buy food, and after I ordered two cheese slices to go, he refused. He put the slices in the oven to heat them up, but he insisted I stay. For no real reason, I tried to fight against his request. I had nothing else to do at my apartment, but it always feels like the polite thing to refuse a request like that, at least the first few times it's offered.

When I relented, he asked me what I wanted to drink. I picked a bottle of Coke, which he took out and, along with the two slices, set down on the counter next to his daughter.

Then he pulled up a seat next to me. For about an hour, I ate slowly, and he asked me questions about my life, my family, and the places I had been. Sometimes he brought his daughter into the conversation, and she would answer and ask questions. No one else came into the store the whole time we spoke. I was sad when the meal of pizza and Coke ended. At first I had been hungry, but the food quickly became a bridge for me to enter into the lives of this man and his daughter. The three of us sitting there alone, exchanging stories about families and home countries, made me happy.

Those are the kinds of gatherings I love. The small ones, between two or three people. With conversation that waves from banal observations about the world to in-depth intimate ideas about loneliness or what a pizza shop owner hopes for his daughter. *Yes, it's starting to get darker earlier these days. And I hope my daughter can find what makes her happy and that she will give it all her effort.*

I wouldn't consider myself an introvert, partly because it seems silly to divide the complexity of the self into such binary categories but also because I enjoy being around larger crowds. Both the large and the small exhaust me. The difference is that one does it at a greater level than the other. I need to constantly remind myself to engage with both, to invite people over or to go to them, because the temptation of solitude is so strong for me that without thinking of it, I can find myself alone for weeks and months. There have been entire days at home where I didn't see my parents, who were only just downstairs.

I have to remind myself that this behavior is neither good nor romantic, that a person is not elevated for wanting or needing to be alone. I tell myself to go downstairs and sit with my parents, to laugh and talk with them, to watch television, to help them out with work or errands. The same way that I tell myself to text friends, to invite them over for lunch, dinner, or a walk, to go to events with them, and to fight the urge to withdraw—no matter how painful and exhausting the resistance is in the immediate present—not only for myself, because all the days alone bleed into each other and have no distinctive features, but also for the people I care about. Relationships need to be nurtured, and for me there is a shame in indulging in myself and my aloneness as the days pass and there are fewer and fewer chances to be with others.

Which is not to say that I have solved the problem. No, I know the medicine, but the aloneness remains. My word processor wishes to change "aloneness" into "loneliness," but they are not the same. There is no pain to aloneness, no isolation from others except that which one chooses. I am not lonely, but I can become addicted to being alone.

My father is most alive among groups of people, emceeing parties or sitting around with the men of the village, sharing stories about the past. When he's back in Nigeria, he can barely go a day without being around people. That is what he loves. When he has to work until late at night as a teacher in the States, having to be in spiritual isolation, he wears his loneliness openly. At the risk of reducing him even further, it seems that in our reflection of one other, we are flipped.

I enjoy smaller gatherings more because the performance of self in them is less extreme. Life itself is a performance, and there's no need to pretend otherwise. There's an old video of Bernard Stiegler I used to love that ends with him declaring that it's not a matter of whether life is a performance or not, because it is, but how good you can make that performance. In large groups, I feel like an actor on stage wearing a mask in front of thousands of other people. The mask is necessary for many reasons, including the need to hide the shame of the performance itself.

My performance cannot be good in large groups, or rather it can't last long, because it takes such a short time before the truth overwhelms me. It is a truth captured in the first few lines of the famous Czeslaw Milosz poem, "Not Mine," as translated by Robert Hass: "All my life to pretend this world of theirs is mine / And to know such pretending is disgraceful." Once I feel it, I can't go on. I either go home or find some corner to watch others from. At that point I become useless. My answers to questions will be dull, and though my friends know that nothing is wrong in the grand sense, those who don't have often interpreted my removal as something aggressive or moody, when it's really just the social and spiritual equivalent of me substituting myself off the field. I would like to keep playing, but I can feel in my body I'm incapable of finishing the match.

The feeling is no different in sport than it is in these social situations. When I was training in Turkey, the coaches would have individual meetings with players where they analyzed our strengths and weaknesses and gave us direction on how to improve. A very standard practice. In one of my first meetings, one of the coaches played the first few minutes of my practices and matches, and he said it seemed like it took me about five to ten minutes before I got into the match. He said it looked as if I wanted to be somewhere else.

In smaller settings, this feeling is less extreme. It exists but it doesn't overwhelm me. Part of the reason is that there is more space between two or three people—space for deeper conversations but also space for quietness. A quietness that is often without anxiety, that doesn't need to be filled. A quietness that can't truly exist in larger groups.

In my time with the pizza shop owner and his daughter, between the banal and intimate topics we covered, we would be quiet, with the only sounds being those from the outside world, the creaking of the stool as the daughter twisted on it, my chewing of the pizza, and the sounds of the man shuffling things around the shop, preparing for the other customers who never came. In these kinds of moments, the feeling that their world was not mine still came, but it could easily be replaced with a more important one: the feeling that it was nice to be around these people. That it made me happy. Watching the day turn to evening with them filled my life with a joy I will never forget, a joy that wouldn't have been there for me if I had immediately returned to the apartment to sit and drink tea alone at the table by the window. Those are the moments I want to last as long as possible. What would bring me joy in the afterlife, if such a thing is possible, is not a full funeral with all of my friends and family but those who will gather afterward, alone with my spirit or with others, to sit and tell stories about the world that I'm truly no longer a part of, or to bring a semblance of my life back through stories of the nonsense that we went through together. Yes, that seems like eternal happiness. To be brought back, in however limited a way, and be able to speak with friends like that again.

When I was done with my food, I left the pizza shop. I hesitated at the door and said goodbyes a few times, promising to visit again. I should have hesitated more and stayed longer. Most of the other times I returned to the area, the shop was closed, with one of those metal gates pulled down in front of it so that I couldn't even see the inside of the shop. I only saw the man and his daughter once again, a few days after the first time, but for some reason I can't remember now, I was in a hurry to the apartment—probably for work and to help my parents, maybe to be by myself. I waved as I walked past, and they waved back. That was it. I never saw them again after that.

On that particular walk back, not knowing it would be the last time I would see them, I noticed the Libreria Toletta, as clear as day on Sacca della Toletta. It was so obvious that I stopped in front of it, wondering how I could have possibly walked past a bookstore so many times without noticing it or going inside. For the moment, I forgot whatever was pulling me back to the apartment and went in. There was an extensive English section as well as an Italian section, but I felt an anxiety in being one of the only people there, so I grabbed a book by Borges and, like any writer, two notebooks, as if the buying of more notebooks would lead to more and better writing.

When I went to pay for the book and the notebooks, I used my card because I hadn't gone to the ATM to get more cash. The machine rejected the card—once, twice, and a third time that made things awkward for me and the cashier. She looked at me with the kind of look every poor person knows and that kills you inside, a look of pity.

She could not make money appear on the card, which the machine was saying was not there. There was money on the card, and I knew it was just a problem of my bank not knowing that I was in Venice, thus rejecting the purchase as fraudulent. But explaining that would have been more pathetic than illuminating.

There are so many humiliations to poverty, some which stick with people throughout their lives, even after their situation changes for the better. That feeling of having a card rejected, of not having enough money at the counter, of having to put back items that can't be afforded, the look from the workers, the impatience of those waiting behind you, that sinking embarrassment and loneliness of being in the spotlight for being poor. No matter how much money I have, a card reader taking longer than usual to approve a purchase brings those feelings all over again.

I could have simply given the book and notebooks back, explained the situation, and come back at a later time. But I wanted to prove to the worker that I wasn't poor; I wanted to distance myself from what I had been before. I told her I would be back, leaving my phone on the counter as collateral, and then ran outside to look for an ATM. When I returned, I gave her a fifty-euro bill, not only to show her that I had money but that I had more than enough of it. I walked out with my change and the three books, not satisfied but feeling shameful at what I had done. That was the first and last time I entered the bookstore. Every other time I walked past it, I looked at the books from the outside and felt the same shame again.

8

During the early days of the pandemic, a professor friend of mine, Ben, asked if I would be interested in being part of a weekly online event he was thinking of hosting. It would be a get together like so many other people were having at the time, except the difference would be that most of the people there would not know each other. We would all only have Ben in common. It wasn't a social experiment, just his way of bringing together and connecting people he valued in his life, a way to pass the time—at least one day a week—with good conversation and whiskey. I agreed to it, not knowing what or who to expect.

The first meeting we had was fairly introductory. In some way, it centered around our collective amazement at how expansive Ben's world was, at the different kinds of people he knew and was able to bring together. There were other professors, a MacArthur genius, a former professional football player, high-ranking media people, and entrepreneurs. There's always some nervousness and strangeness to meeting a friend's other friends. A feeling that these new people may not like you or that you may not like them. And the childlike realization that your friend not only has an existence outside of the relationship they share with you but that they exist in different ways, as different selves, with others—that as well as you may know them, you never really know them as well as you think. Meeting a friend's other friends is a chance to meet the other versions of your friend, which both brings you closer to them while establishing or reestablishing the great distance that exists between the two of you.

I was the youngest member in this new group of friends, and, as I quickly gleaned from the introductions, the least accomplished. This wasn't an issue. The meeting presented no hierarchy, and no one dominated in any way that suggested they needed to be above others. And being the least member of the group, in a sense, is a great way to become a witness, the one who can stand to the side and take stock of the event. It's the opposite of being the host, the person who knows everyone else and the gathering's various dynamics so well that he's responsible for making connections, changing directions in the conversation when necessary, and making sure each individual feels comfortable enough to give their input. The smallest, without having to do much, can see the circle of friends from the edge of the line, which is simply a different place to look from, one in which the benefit of being able to observe better is exchanged for the comfort of being more involved.

Ben noticed this quickly, and he and I began to have a separate conversation of our own at the end of each meeting. Once everyone else logged off, we would talk about the event from our opposite sides, comparing notes and appreciations before going into our own personal updates and more intimate conversations about the same topics we'd covered with the larger group.

Our meetups went on for about a year, and though some people dropped off, the ones who remained naturally grew closer. Tuesday nights became the center of the week, a time for new friends to learn more about each other and talk about the world on fire around them. We spent hours on everything from reclaiming the color red as politically radical to trying to come up with a name for my cat, who I have never addressed by one. The week before I left for Venice, our meeting was a kind of send-off and a time to share stories about travel. One of the people there, David, who was also a professor, asked if I would like to be introduced to a former student of his, Simon, who was a Venetian professor and historian. The next day he made the introduction through email, and Simon was one of the first people I contacted when I had settled in.

Simon was also heavily accomplished, a professor of modern European and Jewish history at numerous esteemed institutions, with numerous degrees, fellowships, and important books to his name. He was a native Venetian whose family had a long history on the island city, and one of the jokes he made was about the pride his family and others from the island feel about being from and living there. He said those on the island have such a sour relationship with mainlanders that it sometimes felt like his family would have liked it better if he had married someone outside of Venice completely than to marry someone from the mainland.

Simon was a wonderful guide to the city. The first time we met up, and a few more times after that, he walked me around, giving almost a block-by-block history of everything we passed. In between, the two of us would talk about our respective lives and histories, share our admiration of David, and discuss the topics of anti-Semitism and fascism, which Simon was an expert on. A great relief in meeting a friend through another friend is that the one who introduced the two of you can always be a point of return in conversation, a bridge to create some familiarity, and because David is such a wonderful man, at least to both Simon and me, the more we returned to our admiration of him, the warmer the rest of our conversation became.

Our first meeting was on the Friday after the US presidential election. In our introductory emails and texts the week before, we said we'd either be meeting in celebration or despair, both situations perfect for some daytime drinking. He asked me to meet him at Campo S. S. Apostoli, which was in the Cannaregio district. When I arrived, there were more people around than I had imagined there would be.

It was more crowded than anywhere else I had been except for Piazzale Roma. Not knowing what Simon looked like in person, I sat down by the old well outside the church and emailed him that I was there and would be easily noticeable, as I would be wearing a bright yellow coat. Soon after, he called out to me, and we greeted each other warmly, both of us almost going in for a hug before stopping ourselves. Then we began walking.

We stopped at a restaurant called Orient Experience. We sat at one of the tables outside. Simon crossed his legs, and like a child mimicking the behavior of adults, I crossed my legs as well. When the waiter arrived, he put down two menus, both in Italian, and Simon, intercepting or anticipating my request, asked the man in Italian to bring an English menu as well. He and the waiter looked at me and laughed, and I smiled apologetically. Simon and I both ordered coffee as well as Aperol spritzes. He told me there was also an Orient Experience II, which was at Santa Margherita, not too far from where I was staying. There was also an Africa Experience that was close to me as well. Whereas Orient Experience served mainly Middle Eastern food, Africa Experience served African cuisine—a hilarious, ambitious, but particularly understandable abstraction for both regions.

The restaurant chain had been started by an Afghan filmmaker who had arrived to present a documentary in

Venice and had sought asylum in Italy. In his almost one
year of living in one of the reception centers near the city, he
began to work and make connections between the refugees
and the students at Ca' Foscari University. The city council
then invited him to work as a linguistic and cultural mediator.
In that role, he ran programming for refugees, including
a festival that required him to collaborate with them on a
menu for the event.

The aim of the menu was to reflect the backgrounds
of the different individuals who helped make it, and this
became the basis of the actual menus that are now used at
the restaurants. With many of the refugees, especially the
minors who were soon to be adults and would thus need to
find work, the idea of a restaurant took shape. It was also
propelled by the fact that refugees were only allowed to be in
the reception centers for up to eight months. The restaurant's
first iteration was a takeout space, but then it became several
establishments where one could sit and eat fairly cheap foods
from Africa and the Middle East. Most of the workers were
recruited through the reception center, regardless of if they
had experience at restaurants, as a way to help transition
them into at least a dignified, working life in Venice.

If I remember correctly, I ordered the Kabuli, which was
only five euros, and a soft drink. Simon and I were meeting
in the middle of the day, when he was taking a break from

schoolwork and working on a book, but we were in no rush. When we were done, he took me on the second leg of our tour, where we crossed the Ponte de Gheto Novo and he showed me the original place where the Jewish ghettos had been. There seemed to be some small construction happening there. He showed me the different synagogues, which are no longer in use, that had existed for different ethnic identities. He said that a few years prior, a performance of *The Merchant of Venice* had been held in the ghetto's main square. It was the first time it had been performed there, even though it's the setting of the play. As we left, I asked him how many Jews still lived in the area, and though he didn't give an exact figure, it was in the hundreds. He said the number had dwindled even more recently because of how expensive it had become. That was similar to the story of the island itself. Just above fifty thousand Venetians were still living there, a number that felt much smaller as we walked and he marveled at the strangeness of having so much space to maneuver.

At the end of our walks, we usually ended up somewhere that looked vaguely familiar to me but which I couldn't be sure that I knew. Part of that was due to how similar the spaces in Venice looked and felt, how easy it was to get confused by the turns, the bridges, and the sudden roads that opened up on the sides, and also because on our walks, I enjoyed listening to Simon so much. I cared less about retaining the

specific information he was giving to me and more about
savoring the joy of each step and his kindness and generosity.
The end of each walk was a small heartbreak, and even with
the promise of another lunch or dinner in the future, I could
feel the ending of our meetings coming with the ending of
my time there. Like David, Simon was unusually gracious
and generous with his knowledge and time in a way that
initially felt suspicious to someone like me, who had grown
up having to be on guard around other people. He was easy
to talk to and be friends with, and I was grateful to spend
some of the days during that terrifying time with him, just as
I was with David and the rest of the group in those Tuesday
night meetings.

When Simon and I ate and walked, there would naturally
be gaps of quiet in the conversation, and sometimes he would
say, to me and as an observation of amazement, that I was
in Venice at such a fantastical time. I was seeing the city in a
way that most Venetians had never seen it before, including
the happiness and calm we could see in the people who
extended kindnesses to one another within the limitations
and horrors of the time, but also in the anxiety and fear that
accompanied the closing of businesses and hotels, and the
stories from business owners who were not sure how they
would survive the pandemic. A place that was shaped to
rely on tourism suddenly losing that has its victories, and

many people had been advocating against the destructions of tourism, but without a transition period, without a concrete plan and some experimentation on how to exist otherwise, the suddenness of the tourists' disappearance put many people who lived and worked in Venice in an extremely precarious position. The water was clearer, there was more space, and people could sit around smoking, laughing, and watching the boats drive by, but in passing a group of gondoliers who had no one to entice and transport, the sadness and tragedy of the fantastical time was also obvious.

At the end of our walks, Simon would also ask me if I knew how to get back to my apartment from where we were. I would say yes even when I didn't. Sensing that, he would give quick instructions about how easy it was to get back. Then I followed his instructions faithfully, whether it was going down certain roads and being careful of forks in the streets or times when the street changed names without warning, or simply taking a water bus back to the Salute stop and going home from the basilica.

The second time he invited me out for lunch was at Santa Margherita to show me the second Orient Experience. The menu was practically the same, but this one had its own unique personality. It was split into two buildings. The small one on the left looked like a diner with tall tables and a lineup of the different available foods: rice, chicken, beef, lamb, and so on. The food was behind a clear glass sneeze guard. In a small hallway behind the counter, essentially the takeout space, Simon notified me that the restaurant was one of the few places in the city allowed to stay open at night. Until 11:00 p.m., the orange glow of its light would stay on, standing out even more in the emptiness and darkness of Santa Margherita and Venice in the winter. The building on the right was the restaurant, with all the elements of the first Orient Experience, except with more space.

I ordered the same thing I had ordered previously, and Simon made a comment that I should be more adventurous. It was Orient Experience, after all, but I was only eating one thing. I tried to explain to him that I'm not an adventurous eater, that all I need to do is find the few things that I like and then stick with them for as long as I can. But in the end, I simply said I liked the Kabuli a lot, and the manager, who had brought our menus and taken our orders, agreed that it was delicious.

Though the manager, who was Middle Eastern, brought out the menus, our waiter for the day was someone different. He was a tall, dark, slender young African man. At first I thought he was Senegalese. I thought this only because Senegalese people are some of the most frustrating people in the world; this is a tremendous generalization and purely personal perception, but they're gorgeous and elegant and seem to carry that beauty with an air of nonchalance. They seem to have a secureness that is wonderful and puts physical looks where they should be, as something for the eyes that can be elevated by an inner elegance.

When the waiter brought our drinks, he and I shared a look of commonality, the way one would shoot a quick glance to a friend across the room at a party. We were the two darkest people in the space, and though we couldn't sit down and share stories during lunch, his presence at the restaurant made me happy. It was lovely to see Simon again, of course, but there was a different comfort that came with someone who looked like me around. Simon and I ate and talked, and then afterward, he showed me the restaurants around the area and walked me to another place that felt unknown. I made my way home from there.

9

With the addition of Simon, Orient Experience II, and Santa Margherita, the rough outlines of the rest of my days in Venice were set. In the mornings, I walked around Dorsoduro. Sometimes I walked toward Piazzale Roma, never reaching it again but deviating slightly off the path to feel the nervousness that comes with being lost and then the excitement of the familiar once I found my way back.

I ventured around the Basilica di Santa Maria della Salute, which had its own sort of small island—for me it was the main attraction—and was separated from me by a three-minute walk, a tunnel, and a small bridge. The Punta della Dogana next to it was closed, as were the other businesses and spaces, like the ENGIM Venezia and the Istituto Marinelli Fonte. All I could do was take a long walk around, go into the church, which had a sign at the front saying it was free to enter and to beware of anyone charging money, or eat at one of the restaurants on the other side of it. Down the Fondamenta Salute were a line of gondolas and an old boat that looked like a merchant ship. In the dark, it swayed so heavily that the mast would clang loudly from parts of the sails hitting it; at night, with the fog, it felt like a warning or the announcement of something important. Since it was docked every time I walked by it, I imagined the sound was a sort of cry from the ship, a lament of its former days of open adventure.

I usually followed the path of Fondamenta Salute all the way down to the tip of the triangle of the island before it diverted backward and sideways to become Fondamenta Zattere Ai Saloni. At the tip was an open space where I would sit to look out and listen to the water. One or two times, there was a young couple there, and the three of us would sit for many minutes without paying too much attention to the other party until either they left or I did, and we would then exchange a wave or a "Ciao."

At the end of my daytime journey, I usually sat on the stairs of the basilica. At the beginning, there were visitors who took pictures from a distance before exploring inside the building. Taking good pictures of the basilica is an impossible task from land. One would have to be on one of the boats arriving at the stop in order to get a great image of it, primarily because it's so grand and the piece of land in front of it is so small that even if a person was standing right on the edge of the water bus stop, which goes into the water, a phone's camera would still either be unable to get the full height and width of it, or it would greatly distort it, making the image so disappointing compared to the real thing that it would simply be better in one's memory. It's more than just the dome, the bell towers, and the four evangelists. The shape of it all—at least the way I appreciated it—needs to be seen up close, with every gorgeous detail, so that it is impossible to see most of it at all, so that one feels small next to it. This makes it hard to grasp, and this larger-than-self aspect elevates the wonder. At least it did for me, and it is one of the reasons why I would sit on the steps and look back every now and then to glimpse something else about it and feel fed through my eyes and heart by the small bite I had taken of it that day. Then the next day, I would look at another section of it or return to a part that still fascinated me. The first time I sat on the steps, I searched my phone and looked up pictures people had taken of the basilica, and the more comprehensive they tried to be, the worse the images were. Or maybe all this is a roundabout way for me to say that looking at the pictures, as filling as they might have been, wasn't enough. What seemed most important was the basilica's grand feeling, the feeling of being small and overwhelmed by it—both the beauty and the size—the sense of awe it created, like being close at the foot of a mountain, where one can do little but acknowledge that this thing before you is much bigger, in the physical and existential sense, than you are.

By late November, when the weather became unbearably dreary, wet, and foggy, those other people disappeared, and I was left alone by the basilica stairs. Even when my daily walk took me elsewhere, I always tried to end it there, sometimes carrying snacks and a drink to enjoy in the dark before going

back to the apartment to work and help my parents from
thousands of miles away.

I believe Simon was the first person to give me a small
insight into the history of the Salute. It was built as a
commemoration to the ending of the black plague, which
had wiped out almost a third of Venice's population at the
time—around fifty thousand people. A handful of times, I
went in. The inside was octagonal, and the path one was
supposed to walk went counterclockwise, with the exit being
the second set of doors to the left of the entrance. There
were arrows and a sign at the entrance and exit—along with
the one about visits being free—that helped ensure visitors
made no mistakes in how they were supposed to experience
it. There were hand sanitizer dispensers on the wall, and also
graphics of footsteps on the ground, similar to the ones at
the entrance of the closed Guggenheim, asking visitors to
stay six feet away from each other.

From the start of the journey to the end were eight chapels,
each with its own beautiful painting. There were three Virgin
Mary paintings by Luca Giordano, along with the Byzantine
Madonna and Child, which sat at the main altar and had
come to Venice after Crete fell to the Ottomans, and Josse
de Corte's statue statute, the *Queen of Heaven Expelling the
Plague*. Tintoretto's *Marriage at Cana* was at the great sacristy,
and Titian's works were everywhere. Whenever I went inside,

there were usually one or two other people walking around quietly, looking at the paintings, taking some pictures, and then exiting within less than five minutes. Except for the pews in front of the high altar at the top of the octagon, it felt more like being inside a museum than a church. The high altar was roped off except during mass, which anyone could attend. Immediately below the rope separating that section of the high altar from the walking path, there was also a small section where you could sit if you wanted to watch the mass without crossing over and participating in it. All but once, I walked around, looked at the paintings, and lit a candle or two in front of one of the altars of the Virgin Mary. Then, after I made sure no one was around me, I said a prayer of protection for my family, and then one more for the pandemic to end.

I was there once during mass. I sat in a seat across from the pews and high altar. I had been to mass many times before, both in Nigeria and the United States. I inherited Catholicism like many other Igbo Nigerians, and my father, who had at one time considered the priesthood, still can recite prayers and verses in Latin. In the village, our church was right across the road from our house. On Sundays, one simply had to cross the street and try not to get their outfit for the Lord dirty in the sand. I still remember my father going up to lead the church in prayer, and the joy of us children sprinting outside once mass was over. The last time I was in that church opposite our house was when we went home to Nigeria before the pandemic. We went in August, which coincided with the anniversary of my grandfather's death. My father held a large commemoration that day, which included attending mass, some native rituals, and also the killing and eating of the largest cattle we could find. That night as we ate, I mentioned to my father that I remembered playing on my grandfather's tomb as a child. The tomb was sort of this sarcophagus that stood in front of our house, the first greeting anyone would receive coming to visit us, and it was so extraordinary and banal that we could play and eat on top of it without forgetting what it was. When my father built our new house in Nigeria, he had the tomb moved to create space.

When the priest at the basilica came out, I saw he was a Black man, a dark African man. I was so surprised that I almost stood up. There were a few people sitting in the pews, but none of them seemed to react to this detail that was particularly unusual to me. The surprising nature of it, of course, was that in Venice at the time—at least in the parts of the city I saw on my walks around—there were hardly any Black people. I saw a few every now and then, including the server at Orient Experience II. There were also probably those who lived just outside of my limited view of the city.

But it was still a shock for me that the priest was Black. I sat through mass focused on him the whole time.

When I went home that night, I researched why there was a Black priest in such an important Venetian church, in Italy, a country infamous for its cruelty to migrating Africans. Cruelty is even putting it lightly; the word that came to me first was "evil." Desperate people drown at sea and it's called "border maintenance." It seemed contradictory to me that a place that could force people to their deaths could then have a person who looked just like the ones they had killed, and who had come from the same country some of those people had come from, as the leader of one of its most famous churches.

The answer to my strange encounter was immediate. There was a shortage of Catholic priests in Europe. Priests were dwindling everywhere, but the problem seemed to be particularly stark there. This made for a peculiar problem, where Africa's priests were being imported to Europe to make up for the shortage, which angered both African churches and traditionalists in Europe.

In a 2019 letter in the *Tablet,* a weekly Catholic publication, which was then republished in the *Telegraph*, Rev. Deacon Michael Phelan, a retired permanent deacon in the diocese of Northampton, wrote, "At a time when this country is extremely short of priests it is disconcerting that our Cardinal and bishops see it as a solution to rob dioceses in Africa and elsewhere of their equally scarce resources of priests." Naturally, he also added: "This leads to our laity having many foreign priests with poor English or accents that cannot be understood, coupled with very different cultural backgrounds."

The Black priest was leading mass at the Salute as part of a continuation of the same relationship of extraction European countries have had with African countries for centuries. It was the same old story. He was necessary and exceptional in the sense that they needed his services. He was conditionally welcomed, while other people who looked like him and me, who were not priests or writers, were brutalized, sent back, or left to die at sea. Not that those conditional welcomes— either his or mine—were anything to celebrate. What is true of exceptions is that when you become like anyone else, when you falter from being special, your privileges can quickly be revoked and you can be condemned to their same terrible fate. In a personal sense, it's a fate much worse because, once, you believed yourself better than the others, or at least luckier. You believed in the lies that no one else did. But in that position as the exception you must permanently behave according to the standards of your masters. You must be their clown and weapon. It's a false citizenship, not a true welcoming or freedom.

10

I only went to San Marco a handful of times, once to meet Simon, another time with a second friend, Ethan, a photographer from the States who was also doing a residency at the time, and a few more times to buy cheap bottles of wine or to sit on the stairs of the Venice Santa Lucia station, which were much larger than the ones in front of the Salute but much less intimate. Both sets of stairs looked out onto the water, but even during the time when so few people were traveling, the train station was full—understandably, even more than the international airport.

When I wasn't walking around the basilica or on the path to Piazzale Roma, I went toward Santa Margherita. On the way was a grocery store at the juncture, I believe, of Rio Terrà Foscarini and Calle Nuova Sant'Agnese. I remember it being at some point before the gallery that had an ATM on the side of it. The grocery store quickly became my rest point on the way back from the walks to either Santa Margherita or toward Piazzale Roma. The first time I went in, I bought a few bottles of Gatorade, a bottle of Fanta, vanilla wafers, frozen sandwiches—mainly tuna and a few others I wanted to be adventurous with and immediately regretted—and two bottles of prosecco. At the register was an Asian man, who I would later find out ran the store with his wife. He was watching a show on his phone, something he would repeat each time I encountered him at the store. He hardly ever glanced up from the show or the football match that had his attention, though he was always cordial and quick in his process.

Naturally, he spoke to me in Italian after scanning my items. He told me the price, which I didn't understand, but thankfully, I could read the amount on the cash register display. Then, as I was getting my card out, he said, "Sacchetto?" And just like the pizza man asking me how many slices I wanted, I was frozen by ignorance. After some silence, he repeated it again, probably thinking I hadn't heard his question. I had, I just had no idea what he was asking. So I stood there again as I had in front of the man at the pizza shop until he glanced up and, reading the silence, pulled out a bag from under the counter and repeated the word again. I nodded my head yes. He bagged everything and handed it to me, and with the groceries in hand, I tried to pay with my card. The machine processed and processed and processed the card, with the same familiar dots on the screen lighting up one by one, asking me to wait for what seemed like an eternity, and the longer it took, the more the terror grew. I stared as if I could will it to approve the payment, as if I could convince it to have some compassion and mercy to save me from embarrassment. But a machine is a machine, and it can only do what it is programmed to. My card was declined again—

the same familiar words of rejection, the same deflating and unforgettable sound of disapproval. Standing there in front of the manager, bag in hand, a small part of me wanted to run out of the store. But I would have betrayed my father if I had.

As I did at the Libreria Toletta, I asked the man to give me a moment. Then I ran outside to find the nearest ATM, which was just next door, and after getting out a fifty-euro bill, I returned and held it up to him triumphantly, as if to prove that I hadn't run away and that I had the necessary money. The man, who must have dealt with situations like this an innumerable amount of times, took the money, gave me my change, and went back to his show without making a fuss or showing any appreciation for what had occurred. It was another day at work for him, and I was a customer like anyone else.

Among the rules that my father had for our family, there were a few that were nonnegotiable. Because my grandfather was killed by poisoning, we didn't eat or drink at other people's houses. We were also forbidden to steal, no matter how little we had. This covered stealing from other people but also stealing from stores, corporations, and the like.

Being forbidden to steal from other people made sense to me, at least in the cases of stealing from those who were as unfortunate or less fortunate than you. Not taking the little from those with nothing was understandable, even as I knew the pull of the opportunity and the misery that drives the behavior. But I am more in line with Wilhelm Reich when it comes to taking food and other necessities that are abundant but that the poor are barred from unless they can pay for them, even as they starve outside the doors of stores and corporations. When it comes to stealing laterally, there's always a balance of feeling in those cases, of knowing that poverty is a man-made evil, one that not only humiliates but constricts life in such vicious ways that it can reduce a person to living only in order to get to the next day, while those who have more, mainly from the privilege of being born lucky, by pure chance—which they refashion into a heroic story about how exceptional they are—spew nonsense about overcoming the suffocating conditions of poverty through hard work, determination, and other empty words that all but suggest that those who are condemned to poverty and who find no way out of it are lazy, unambitious, and, at the heart of it, morally inferior. As if the poor aren't the ones who are worked to death. As if it's not the poor who have to constantly decide to sacrifice their lives to the drudgery of so much meaningless work, smiling through the daily aggressions of their supervisors and their customers in order to one day leave a better foundation for their children. As if the poor have time.

Of all the things poverty can take from someone, including the simple desire to live a dignified life, the lack of time is especially frustrating. There's never any time. No time for life. No time to do anything but work and recover and work again. No time left but to add more work in order to make the money that will supposedly grant time in the future, a future you must believe in even as the money never seems sufficient and the time never comes. That is not to say that the lives of the poor are without joys and depth. Even now when I think of the times I was poor, I remember so much of the happiness, but within its confines, you can feel each second slipping, each moment painfully grinding away.

There are many stories I could tell about my own struggles with being poor, this tragedy of lost time, but the deep anger that still exists in me now came from watching my father deal with it. It would be another injustice to my parents now to say they were poor; both of them would deny it and would be right in their denial. My mother, having six children who were always fed and taken care of, never saw herself as poor. Her personal worldview was the same as Niobe's: her children are her wealth. There are six of us, but only because we were poor when we moved to the States. After having my youngest brother—the only one of us born in the US—the cost for having a child here was so high, and it was so difficult to raise children because both my parents also had to work and go to school, my mother decided that six was enough. Yet she still talks about how she wishes she had eight.

Once, at a Nigerian party in Detroit, one of my mother's "friends" came over to the table where my mother and I were sitting. I say "friend," though I mean she was just another Nigerian woman in the community; they must all interact and be friendly in public, though there's rivalry, envy, and meanness that's obvious to anyone who has ever been to one of these gatherings. After the squealed greetings and exchanged hugs, the woman talked for some time about all the good things that had happened to her recently, from moving to a big home in the suburbs to all of the cars she and her husband owned. She talked about all of this while contrasting her wealth with our family's situation, making small references to how dangerous our neighborhood was for them, or to how she used to own a car like my mother's— all in that friendly tone that is much more insulting than if someone said they hated you outright. Once the faux-friendly conversation was done, I asked my mother how she could stand such insults. She laughed and said that the other woman only had two children; she had nothing that my mother wanted. The younger me, being so fixated on the humiliation of the encounter, saw my mother's response as a coping mechanism, but that is actually who she is. She cries each time any one of us leaves, whether we are going away for a week or moving out permanently. And most nights, unless one of us is traveling internationally, she curls up on the living room couch and calls us one by one. When I watched Chantal Akerman's first film, *News from Home*, where Akerman reads the sweet and painful messages her mother sent her while she was studying in New York City, it felt like I was watching a film about my own mother.

This is not to say that the effects of our poverty did not reach her. It was impossible for them not to. Poverty is pressure, and it intensifies every little problem into a big one, and every big problem into something existential. She felt poverty's effects, and she suffered in her own way. But she also had a great consolation and focus. As long as her six children were healthy and happy, she saw herself as richer than the gods.

In my father's case, though, the responsibility for his children weighed heavily on him. When my parents reached retirement age, I kept insisting that they give up on working since they have both worked nonstop for over three decades. My mother said she would, but my father refused. They had only recently started saving money because my father saw no purpose in them putting money away earlier, when it could go to the children for necessities or other activities, sports, or dreams we were pursuing. My father was against stealing, but he would swallow his pride to sell his father's land and ask for money if it meant a better life for his children.

Because my father was the most dominating and domineering figure in my life when I was young, I used to blame him for our poverty and the anger I had because of it. I saw what all of my friends had. The friends who didn't have much but had more than we did. Friends whose parents drove newer cars. Friends who went to the movies regularly, who went to the mall and wore popular shoes. Friends who played Game Boys, Nintendo 64s, Dreamcasts, PlayStations, Xboxes. Friends whose houses I would visit and feel small in their bigger kitchens, bedrooms, and garages. I blamed my father for all of it. He didn't do enough. He wasn't doing enough. Other people had parents who worked jobs that paid them well, but my father decided to do odd jobs—selling wine or selling ice cream—before becoming a full-time teacher again. Teaching was what he knew, what he liked, and where he felt most responsible and most respected. Or it used to be. In the States, teaching was different. I blamed him for doing something that I could see made him miserable and that paid very little, for choosing stability over the possibility of something new, something better, something more respectable. Someone had to be responsible for the conditions my family was in, and I chose my father. He didn't choose for us to be at the bottom, but in my eyes, he kept us there.

What I couldn't see then was that being poor was crushing him much more than me. Still believing I was the center of the world and that my pain was the most significant, I couldn't see the obvious truth before me. He was shouldering a responsibility that was large enough to get him through the daily humiliations but that took away his precious time and other possibilities in life. He wanted to be at home in Nigeria—those dreams of going into politics that still keep him watching political news every night, he gave up for us. What he wanted to be for us in the States was our foundation, a great tree not in size but one that survives and allows its seeds to rise up higher and grow wider than it could by starving itself and giving its food to those seeds. And the great price he paid wasn't just the daily humiliations but all of the time in his life.

One of the earliest and strongest memories I have of our first few years in the States is watching my father walk to work at night from the window of the one-bedroom that we stayed in at the house on Clements Street. I can see him clearly now, with his long black Raiders jacket. I feel now, after all of these years, what I felt then as a child: This is my father, who is superhuman. But back then, I couldn't see the effects of all of those nights on him.

My mother could deal with the insults about the little we had because she saw herself as richer through her children.

But my father felt every insult as a judgment and personal condemnation. I've seen him and been with him as he's been insulted by so many people, from others in the Nigerian community of Detroit, to his colleagues and superiors, to normal Americans who spoke to him as if he was an inconsequential foreigner. I know the look on his face when he's holding his anger in, and I know the look on his face when he's heartbroken and hurt but can't show it. It's the same look he has when I leave for a trip or go back to New York City after visiting. My mother will cry, but my father will stand around with a forced smile because he doesn't know what to do with himself. And sometimes he won't look at me—he'll look off into the distance.

Since those days of walking to Rite Aid, my father has worked relentlessly. He has never taken a vacation, and he takes on extra work whenever he can in order to make a little more money. My mother has enough resistance and reason to sometimes say she doesn't need to work anymore after-school activities, at least for a year or two, because she should at least have time to rest at the end of a workday. But still today, as has been the case since I was in high school, my father doesn't get home until 9:00 or 10:00 p.m. during the school year. He has six children, and siblings and their children back in Nigeria who ask so much from him, and no matter how angry he gets, he can't say no to those who need him. That is his life. And he pays for this faithfulness with time and his body. When he gets home these days, he lays on the bed or sits on the floor because there's a fracture in his back that makes it difficult for him to sit comfortably anymore. When he eats, the hand he holds the spoon with shakes. They're tremors—nothing fatal—but his hand shakes from years of stress. Each morning and night, he takes medicine for numerous issues. He is sometimes short of breath. Pressure has built up behind one of his eyes so that my mother or I have to squeeze prescription eye drops into them every day. My father, who was once one of the best athletes in not only our village but in all of the schools, is breaking down because of the work and responsibility he carries. He gave up the other possibilities for his life, and this world is taking his body from him. That was the price he paid.

One of the only trips we've ever taken as a family was to Disney World in Orlando, Florida. It must have been about six years after we moved to the States because the image of that trip that has stayed with me is that of my dazed little brother wiping his eyes from tiredness at the Cleveland bus terminal. We made the journey on a Greyhound bus, and it took fifteen hours each way. Thirty hours to get to and come back from Disney World because my father saw and knew his friends and colleagues were taking their children there, and he didn't want us to miss out. So he saved the little money he had and took his wife and six children from Detroit to Orlando to stay for a few days before returning. After that, he always talked about taking us on a cruise because everyone else did, but the older we got, the more expensive our lives became, and in paying for college tuition for all of us, the money for the cruise never came. There was always a more immediate problem to handle.

11

At the beginning or after each one of my parents' work sessions, or if there were breaks where they didn't need help with a critical issue, I would talk and joke around with them. With my mother I could talk about anything, from the ways that her people pronounce Igbo words differently than people from Imo state, to teasing each other about our looks. In order to stop me from becoming arrogant, she calls me ugly. In response, I tell her I look just like her, so if I'm ugly, then we're in the same boat.

My father and I talked about many things as well. Where my mother long ago accepted that I have no problem walking away from a job when the work feels like it is dominating my life, or when the workplace becomes too stressful, that attitude still makes my father uneasy. He wants me to be happy, but he also wants me, along with my siblings, to be stable. That can mean that he suggests we take work that is available to make sure that we're planning for the future. Sometimes his attitude can be annoying, but it makes sense for him. That is how he's had to live his life, and after what he's sacrificed, he wants to know that when he's gone, his children won't be struggling.

My parents and I talked about work, football, politics, and, in the time I was in Venice and my months at home before then, we talked about the past. The difference between talking about the past with my mother and with my father is that with my father, there's always a lot left unsaid and untouched. Neither of us wants to revisit those spaces between us.

One thing I return to with both of them, but especially with my father, is when we sold ice cream together in the summers. It was an idea that came to my father from a friend who was doing the same, and with my dad looking for ways to supplement the family's income from teaching, and finding out he could potentially make hundreds of dollars each day, my father decided to rent a small ice cream truck.

The truck was a surprise to the family, but the logic was reasonable. The problem was that he needed someone to be with him during those days so he could be responsible for driving while the other person spoke to customers and dealt with the money. He could do both, but having two people made it easier. And of course, because of his heavy accent and the way Americans spoke so quickly, having someone who could understand them better and also speak to them fluently made sense.

My younger siblings were too young to be put in that position, so the only two choices were my older brother and me. My older brother was the first choice because he was the more responsible one but also because he got along much better with my father. They looked alike and had similar attitudes, and being the first son, my older brother was championed in a way I wasn't. But he was also as stubborn as I was. After a few days of waking up at 7:00 a.m. to drive to the ice cream park, he was done. He said, no more. And when my older brother says no, it is a final declaration, not a point of argument.

That left me as the second and last choice. The difference in power between my older brother and me at that time was that when he said no, it was respected. When I said no, it led to punishment, yelling, guilt-tripping, and often my concession to doing what was asked. And after my older brother refused, I became the person to sell ice cream with my father.

My siblings and I usually had a six-week math camp that we went to, and those first few weeks of the summer were the only times in high school I didn't sell ice cream with my father. Once the camp was done, my siblings could enjoy the rest of the break while I went to work.

My father and I woke up early in the mornings each day. Or rather, it's more honest to say that he woke up early and then woke me up so I could get ready for the day. From home, we drove in his red Toyota Camry to the ice cream park, which was this huge building you pass on Greenfield Road on the West Side of Detroit before reaching Dearborn. It had a large parking lot filled with many rows of different-sized white trucks, a store where boxes of different ice creams were sold, and then an open space in the middle, like the working area in an auto repair shop, where dry ice was distributed.

We stood in line and bought the ice cream we needed to replace the flavors that sold the most: strawberry shortcake, cookies and cream, ice cream sandwiches, the big dippers, a few of the bomb pops, all of the ones in cups, and the Spider-Man ice cream. The strawberry shortcake was probably the one that we ran out of the most, so we usually stocked up with several boxes of it. What annoyed me then was that there was a second strawberry ice cream—the sundae crunch bar—which I knew was superior, but people would rarely buy it. Their ignorance was my prize, though, since I would eat most of the ones we bought.

After we bought the ice cream, we bought the ice. This meant my father haggled over the price while I stuck my finger on blocks of dry ice and marveled at the pinching effect it had on my skin. Several times I put my tongue on it and immediately regretted it. But that didn't stop me from doing it again until I felt my father's glare from behind me.

Once we had everything, we mapped out the areas of the city we were going to spend our day in. The West Side was most familiar to me, but since my father had spent years selling wine throughout Detroit and its suburbs, he had a wider range of knowledge of the city than I did. At the beginning we tended to be more adventurous with where we went to sell, sometimes going all the way to Chalmers near the Chandler Park water park. But after years of selling, we had an understanding of which areas were most profitable. We sort of had a claim to certain parts of the West Side, especially down Dexter and Livernois Avenue. The people around those areas knew to expect us every day, and other ice cream trucks avoided it. Everyone had their turf.

At the beginning, our selling day started about 10:00 a.m. and lasted until we ran out of the best ice cream, which was usually around five or six. After the first two summers of selling in the small truck, my father was able to buy his own. It was much larger and had space in the back for a big freezer, which allowed us to stay out until nine.

Each day we drove the truck down the streets of Detroit with one of five available songs playing, songs that are forever stuck in my head. "Pop Goes the Weasel" is the classic ice cream truck song, the one everyone plays. But the song that was intoxicating to kids, or the kids back then, was "Do Your Ears Hang Low?" For some reason, it was like catnip for children. Simply changing the song from something else to "Do Your Ears Hang Low?" would encourage kids to come sprinting out of their houses, forcing their parents to spend money they hadn't planned to and glare at me as if I had reached into their pockets and taken the money out myself.

Those days of selling ice cream were so long, and there

were so many of them, that remembering them now, they all blend together, like one long summer day with the same song playing over and over. Most of the time when I was hungry, I was allowed to eat the ice cream that we had an abundance of, though I could also get away with eating the really good flavors if I wanted to. My father would get annoyed, but he would still allow it. I just had to make sure he knew, because to him, eating it without his awareness was as bad as stealing. My father usually drank a Pepsi and ate cookies and cream or the Neapolitan ice cream sandwiches no one ever wanted. On days we were really hungry, or if we'd had an excellent day and wanted to celebrate, we'd get McDonald's or Burger King.

Certain memories of those days have stayed with me. I remember once when we were driving the truck down Wildemere on the West Side, and my dad was so tired that when he tried to pull over, he hit the brakes too late and tapped the back of the car parked in front of us. The man who owned it was standing there on the sidewalk. For the next few hours, we stayed there, with my father first arguing with the man and then the man calling to speak to his insurance company. I don't think we had insurance on the truck then, which made my father nervous. He paid for the repair with money out of his pocket, and that was money he was saving for his children.

I remember the time we were stopped on Schoolcraft and there was a large gathering of kids—paradise for us. But as we were selling to the crowd, a gunfight started less than a block away. At first there was a stillness, the same sense of time stopping that one feels before a car accident, and then everyone ran. We were in the truck, and in front of us was a dead end, so we pulled over and waited it out until the coast was clear. We drove away from that area but still kept selling. A gunfight wasn't worth giving up the hundreds of dollars we could make that day.

One of the first times I saw my father truly scared, and realized how he hid it in his face though his eyes betrayed him, was when we were coming home during a thunderstorm. The rain was heavy. This wouldn't have been a problem except that the truck had a defective windshield wiper that we kept putting off fixing because it hardly rained, or rained for long, in the summer. But that was the hardest rain I've ever been in. That might not be true—Nigeria, after all, has a rainy season with more violent storms—but it felt like the hardest rain because my father was leaning forward on the steering wheel, trying to see out of any clear space on the windshield he could. Every few minutes or so, he turned to me and made a joke about us being stuck in the rain, or about how the ice cream park seemed farther than usual, but as soon as his face turned toward the road, his eyes flashed this deep sense of worry that made me feel bad for him. If I could have at that time, I would have put my hand on his shoulder to let him know it would be alright. But that was not our relationship.

The most devastating thing that happened to us during that era was the burning of the red Toyota Camry. We were coming back, late as usual, to park the ice cream truck and go home, but as soon as we entered the gates, a bunch of other drivers we knew, Nigerian and otherwise, stopped us and asked us to get out of the truck. We were suspicious. They immediately told my dad to try to stay calm, which naturally made him even more suspicious and anxious. I was so tired. I was just ready to go home. My dad demanded to know what was going on, and they nervously explained that our car had caught on fire.

The young mechanic who serviced the rentals had been working on one that was next to our car, and he accidentally spilled oil underneath our car. That's not a problem on its own. His stupid mistake was that after he was done working, he took out his cigarette and flicked it on the ground next to him. The oil caught on fire right underneath our car. He must have not seen it immediately, or perhaps he had left, because when we went back to look at the Camry, it was unrecognizable. A black skeleton. I walked around it in shock, feeling the damage with my fingers, making sure it was indeed real. My father stood there, unable to speak or comprehend what he was seeing. The words I will never forget him saying—and I don't remember if he said them to anyone in particular or if he simply said them to himself—was him asking how he would drive his kids then.

The paradox of the days of selling ice cream with my father was that even though he and I had never been as close physically, it was also the time that we grew the most distant from one another.

Those summers were the time I realized that my father hated me. The realization came gradually, but there was a moment when it became undeniably clear. We were at home. My father was asleep, and my siblings and I were in the living room, playing video games. My older brother wanted to play, even though it wasn't his turn. He kept asking me to hurry up and give him the controller. I refused. Then he went from asking to trying to take it. Back then, I wasn't afraid to fight him or anyone else; in fact, I was always looking for a reason to do so. He started the fight, but I happily obliged him. My father, hearing the commotion, which woke him up from his much-needed rest, stormed out of his room and, without asking who was in the wrong, pulled me away from my older brother. Before I could even explain, he started hitting me. He hit me over and over. Normally, I would have been able to pull myself away or at least prepare myself, but the beating took me by such surprise that I felt every single hit.

It was my older brother who jumped in to stop it. He pulled me away. And as I stood there confused, with tears rolling down my cheeks, he screamed at my father and admitted that he was the one at fault, that he had started the fight. My father looked at both of us and didn't know what to do. I stared back at him, my chest heaving from the fight and from the punishment. He saw me as the bad child to the extent that without even knowing the situation, he had come after me. And then, after finding out he was wrong, all he could do was stand there and look at me. He didn't say he was sorry. He didn't take me into his arms to console me. He just looked at me.

Standing there, sweating, heaving, and crying, I accepted deep inside my soul that he hated me. Through everything else, part of me thought he still loved me like he had in the village, that he was still the man who had rescued us from the rain, the one who had bought me my first soccer ball, the man who had been overjoyed when I was born. But he wasn't. He truly hated me. That's when I said, no more. He would get no more of me. Nothing. That's what I had for him from then on. No tears ever again. No desire to be loved, no connection. I said nothing to him at that moment. I stared at him and then walked away. And as I went upstairs to my room to run over the pain, I said no to him. No matter what happened, I would never forgive him for the hate he had for me.

So in those days, when we sold ice cream together, we spent most of those hours in silence. I leaned against the window of my seat and looked out. If he didn't ask me to do something, or wasn't speaking to me, I said nothing to him. He must have seen and felt it, but I became so distant to him. The minotaur took the little child who, even in his worst behavior, still wanted to be seen by his father, and to protect him, set him deep inside the labyrinth to never come out again. I became so monstrous afterward. Nothing my father could do from then on would touch me. None of his yelling, his hitting, his threats to send me back to Nigeria had any effect. The more he punished me, the worse I behaved. I wanted to see which one of us would burn up first in our fall together and if he would let go before we hit the ground. I had nothing to lose. I was nothing in his eyes, in the eyes of my teachers, and in the eyes of many other people. It suited me perfectly. I wanted to not be seen as worthwhile so that by starting from zero, I would have the chance to live as I wanted.

Our time selling ice cream came to an end when my mother wanted to help out by renting a truck herself. She usually taught summer school, but in the last summer of my high school years, she wasn't placed in any of the schools and so decided to make money doing what my father and I did. I remember, before that summer, I had received a bad report card to end the year, though I didn't care about it at all. I showed it to my father, and he reacted by yelling and then grabbing his belt to hit me. He swung it the first time, and I put my left arm up to shield it. Then he swung it again, and I caught it. I looked him in the eye and told him enough. That was it. I told him in Igbo, no more. Let me be nothing, but you don't get to hit me anymore.

Because my mother couldn't sell ice cream on her own, my father told me to go with her. I don't remember feeling relief or excitement about it. Back then, I was also angry with her for allowing what happened to me to happen. I was angry at everyone. That's not to say it was a bad time. My mother and I still got along very well in those days.

Every morning before going on our route, we got gas at the Marathon station where Clements Street meets Dexter Avenue. While we were there one morning, she gave me the clear bucket we used for change and asked me to go in the back and count it while she filled up the car. As soon as I sat down, I saw her get pulled out of the truck. She started screaming and crying. Confused, I walked to the front of the truck, carrying the bucket. I saw her being held by two men, and one had a gun to her head. I've never seen my mother more scared than at that moment. I was calm, mostly because the situation was annoying, and after being held at gunpoint and shot at several times, I looked at situations like this with a distance I had given myself inside—I was dulled to what was happening. The man with the gun yelled at me to give him the money. I threw the bucket at him. The second one grabbed it and went through the change. Disappointed, he demanded more, and I told him we didn't have anything because we were just starting our day. Then I sarcastically asked why he thought we were at the gas station to begin with.

The two men recognized they looked silly, and with onlookers crowding around, they let my mother go, grabbed the bucket, and ran away. My mother ran into the gas station crying, and a couple of women gathered around to take care of her. I called my father on her cell phone and told him what had happened. He stopped his route, picked up my older brother from home, and came to us. He drove my mother back home, and my brother and I drove back in my mother's truck. My mother was too traumatized from the event to ever sell ice cream again. I spent the rest of the summer working with my father, and at the end of it, he parked the ice cream truck at the back of our house. He never used it again.

12

Writing about the death of her brother, Andronicus Porphyrogenitus, in the *Alexiad*, princess Anna Komnene tells us:

> But it is wonderful that nowadays nobody is changed, as they say happened in former days, into a stone or bird or tree or some inanimate thing, changing his nature into such things under the force of great calamities; whether it is all a fable or truth. For perhaps it were better to exchange one's nature for another that is non-sentient, than to possess such a vivid perception of evil. If this had been possible, the ills that have befallen me would very likely have turned me into stone.

I was midway through my time in Venice when, after some nudging from Ted and other friends who were annoyed that I was in Venice at such a time yet was not taking advantage of seeing the sights, I decided to visit San Marco alone. The other time I went there was with Ethan. We met at the bridge by the Galleria and then took the boat to San Marco, where we walked around St. Mark's Square. On my journey alone, I used one of the boutique stores—I believe it was Louis Vuitton—as a destination.

I could go on to describe that area of San Marco, with all of its boutiques, international and local, and their display windows of pricey items, some which I liked very much—I will usually stop to look at watches and things made of gold—but the truth is that for me, it seemed like any other shopping area in a big city. There were shops and expensive things to buy. It didn't seem any different or more special than those kinds of areas in London, Paris, Berlin, New York, or Los Angeles. Because there were so few tourists around, there was a dystopian feeling around that area particularly, with the small number of people walking in and out of the shops, mostly in silence, and the workers having to stand at attention, moving and caring for items and stores as if to pretend that the world was the same as before. They still had to perform their roles as service employees, with forced smiles and patience, even as the hours went by with only one or two people coming in, looking at some items, and then walking out without buying anything. Everyone seemed lost. The normal way of things had been broken, yet in this post-world, there seemed to still be this pretense to go about things as before. In Venice, this performance seemed heightened in San Marco where, beyond anything else, one goes to spend money as a tourist.

There's always an uneasiness for me in these shopping centers of a city. That feeling was clear in Venice considering its identity as a city of commerce and one that survived largely on tourism. The determined way to experience the place, at least for an outsider, is to buy things. To constantly be spending money on everything from expensive global brands to local art. One is a consumer, first and foremost, which often feels like the standard way that the world sees people in this age. One of the last remaining ways that a person is supposed to express themselves to the world. No amount of complaining will change it, but it was especially disturbing having to play that role during a global pandemic.

I floated around the shops in San Marco like a ghost, mostly window-shopping. I wasn't disappointed by the experience but unimpressed. Part of that was the performance of consumerism, but I was also absurdly becoming ridiculously tribal about the superiority of the Dorsoduro to other places in Venice. Simon had laughed at this during one of our lunches, when I confidently stated that it was the best area in the city, as if I had seen and lived everywhere else extensively. My declaration was childish, in the sense that it was similar to how a child might declare that they have the best mother in the world. That's how I felt about the area where I was staying, about the pizza shops, the restaurants, the open spaces, the water bus stops, the grocery store, Campo Santa Margherita, the Salute, the Galleria, the small streets and sharp corners. The more I walked around and experienced them, the more I felt inside that they were the best in all of Venice; I didn't need to see the rest. And when I visited other places, like San Marco, I was already holding onto that great bias, which meant I could only see them as lesser in comparison. There was nothing San Marco could have done to impress me, and even if it had impressed me spectacularly, I would have found another way to reason why it was still beneath what I felt had become my little labyrinth. It was a silly position I held inside, but the silliness of it was fun to hold onto. I wasn't debating with anyone, and no one was arguing with me about it, but somehow, I was still combative about a place that I didn't even belong to. But inside I felt that I had temporarily made a home, even with its faults and my position there as an other, and because of this, I had—compelled only by myself—to take the stance that it was the best home out of all the available ones around.

One thing about Venice at the time was that because of the early closing of the stores, the landscape could change dramatically in a matter of minutes. In San Marco, I went inside a burger shop to begin my routine of looking at the menu with intense focus, as if I had never seen a menu of burgers and fries before, being so indecisive that the workers would give up their facade of politeness and instead look at their phones until I was ready to order. As I looked, I would ask myself whether I really wanted a burger or not.

My heart and stomach said yes, but I was skeptical of this yes. It wasn't strong enough, and eating a burger in Venice seemed undignified. But then of course, there was no other food I felt strongly about. I didn't know what I wanted, and a burger seemed like an easy fix to the situation of hunger and uncertainty. Yet if I got the burger and regretted it, then I wouldn't forgive myself for making such a silly choice. Worse, if I got the burger and it was bad, or my body rejected it, then I would stop eating burgers for an extended amount of time in protest to the bad quality but also to punish my heart and stomach, which had both led me astray. This nonsensical turmoil went on for such a long time that when I finally decided not to get the burger and went back outside, it seemed like everyone had disappeared. There hadn't been that many people around to begin with, but coming outside, it was only me and two or three others, who were disappearing around the corners.

There was nothing left for me to do in San Marco. Being the only person there as it turned to evening made me feel exposed. I was thinking of the worst things that could happen if one of the armed men who patrolled the city saw me walking around when everyone else was inside. Though there weren't any explicit orders—at least in that area—that said people couldn't walk around after curfew, it felt best to avoid any encounters and questions about why I was still outside.

It started to rain. My stomach growled, and as I walked back to the Giglio bus stop, I scolded myself for not getting any food, for declining the opportunity to get the burger—which I couldn't go back and get as a matter of pride—when I walked past Bar Longhi, a waterfront restaurant and bar with incredible views of the Grand Canal and the surrounding landmarks. The doors to the inside were open, and the outside dining area, which was covered and fitted with heaters, was still set up. Another inner argument started. I had to decide whether I wanted to get out of the rain, avoid a potential encounter with an armed patrolman, and get home for work, or if I wanted to take the chance and eat at one of the only restaurants that was still open. I was standing there turning my head back and forth from the restaurant to the bus stop when I decided that enough was enough. I couldn't argue myself into paralysis anymore. I went inside.

There was one waiter, a woman, and a man who seemed like the manager. The woman asked me in English if I wanted to sit outside or inside, and I chose to sit outside. I wanted to look out toward the water and watch the boats speed across it to get out of the rain as quickly as possible.

After she set up the table for me, I ordered an Aperol spritz, because that's what you do in Venice, and, looking at the menu for only a minute or so, decided on the steak in order to stop myself from overthinking. Future consequences be damned. The food came out pretty quickly. When the woman brought the steak, after already bringing the drink and some bread, she then sat two tables ahead of me, outside in the rain, crossed her legs, and lit a cigarette. The two of us sat there in silence. I ate and drank slowly, often being distracted by the rain and the boats. She smoked her cigarette and scrolled through her phone. A few times, she left someone a voice note. Once or twice she asked me how the food was and if I needed anything else. When the wind pushed droplets of rain onto us, we laughed about it and then went back to our individual activities. I sat next to her until a few minutes after 7:00 p.m. that night, and I was sad to be done when I was. I could have sat there longer, and she would have let me. The manager had gone home, and she seemed responsible for closing the restaurant, but she didn't seem to be in any rush and told me to take my time, waiting until I asked for the check to bring it. I drank three spritzes, but she only charged me for one, and when we said our goodbyes, I was a bit sad at the thought that I would never see her again—or rather, that I would not see her in the same context again. The two of us alone in the rain, alone in that part of San Marco, with the dark setting in and the boats bouncing on the water. The time we had there would be the first and last time like that.

I had to get home though. I had people to avoid on the streets, work to do at the apartment, and parents to speak to and help with their own work. The bus ride was wonderfully lonesome, as most of them were then. There were about three of us riding, the last stragglers of the day, each lost in their own thoughts, mesmerized by the dark water underneath and the hypnotic swaying of the boat. When I got off at the Salute stop, I considered walking around the area again. The cold, dark, and rain felt inviting and perfect for a walk alone to think about one's life and the absurdity of the times. A perfect night for a minotaur to haunt the streets. It wouldn't take that long, and I could always come up with an excuse for missing part of one of my endless number of meetings. The only risky thing would be if my mother or father had an urgent problem, but I was willing to test fate in that regard, and in a dark part of myself, I perhaps wanted to be a bit careless with them.

What stopped me was the sound of a familiar string instrument. It must have been playing when I landed, but I didn't hear it until I made the decision to walk around, and the sound instantly pulled me toward the small bridge and tunnel that separated the area of the church from where my apartment was. It felt as if I was floating toward the sound. When I arrived at the tunnel, it was the man in black again, the musician with the old instrument and circular black hat. His case was open in front of him, showing the little money others must have donated, and a few CDs of his music. I wanted to take one of them, but I had no cash on me at the time, and it seemed inconsiderate to ask for his music without paying for it. So instead, I stood in front of him and listened. It was only the two of us in the small tunnel, and he played without looking at me as he had the first time I saw him. The only gesture he made toward me came when I arrived and he looked up, nodded, and then turned his face back down.

Since I don't have a sophisticated enough understanding and language for music, I can't truly describe the sound of the man's song. I imagine any attempt to speak of it in technical terms would only get further away from the feeling of it. What I can say is that the slow and somber tone of his playing reminded me of the sad and heavy tune my father would sometimes hum to himself while writing or lying in bed, and without explanation, all of us in the house would know he was thinking of his siblings and parents who had died. Those he would never see again. So, if I could have, I would have cried in front of the man in black, but because I couldn't, I stood opposite of him in the dark, enjoying the music I also wanted to run away from.

The man in black didn't play for long. I caught him at the end of his night, which made me wonder whether he had been playing there in the dark by himself before I arrived. After about five minutes, he stopped, packed up his guitar, nodded at me again, this time saying, "Ciao," before he walked down C. S. Gregorio and disappeared from view. That was the last time I saw him. As he vanished into the night, I looked around and thought, this is where the minotaur assumes its bodily shape.

I was already a minotaur in spirit, but I needed to be one physically as well. Everything I did in Venice, I did so while imagining for two: for myself and for the minotaur to come. He was with me at every moment. The bodily change was important then, as it is in transformation stories, because it had to serve as a reminder that the body is neither a shell or something divided from the existence of the self or person. It cannot even be regarded as a vessel for the self or person because that designation still implies a separation and distance. I can understand why some people might believe in the division of the body and mind, or the body and spirit, and why the body, with all of its frailties and its susceptibility to the elements, might frighten many people because it reminds them of death, of the tragedy of time passing and the structure of life, which ends inevitably for everyone, an ending signaled first by graying hair and sagging skin before the mind catches up in slowing down. If one is lucky. Because there are probably more unlucky ones who don't get to the end of the road naturally than those who do. And still, their ending is often a reminder of the body's weaknesses.

The fears of the body don't negate what it is, and the zealous determination to escape it doesn't mean that it is not the primary site of life, a miracle in its design and a path for understanding ourselves and the world around us. What I mean is that the body is how life is lived in the material sense. To touch, to feel, to be—it all lives in the body. There is not a moment in life where our bodies are not engaging with the world around it, where we're not being part of that world physically. Even in sitting still, or moving to the outskirts of civilization, to the most desolate and remote places possible, one is still a part of the world through the body.

As a site of understanding the world, we know that not all bodies are considered equal. From skin color to disabilities, visible or otherwise, to the physical performance of gender, there is a history that determines what kinds of struggles one has to deal with because of the body one has been born into. The more marginal those bodies are, the better—or rather the clearer—understanding one gets of the world's true face. In New York, it only took an ankle injury for me to see the cruelty against disabled people that's inherent in the city's architecture. This is not by mistake but rather is a statement about who gets to participate in that society, who gets to be part of that community. Sometimes this statement is made by not having any way for disabled people to access buildings, and sometimes it's done through the violence of borders, laws, societal structures, and long stares as someone walks around that remind them that they are not wanted or welcome. I've said before that I sometimes like to be invisible, but depending on one's body, that possibility is often impossible.

That is also why the transformation into the minotaur had to be physical, to take the otherness to its most extreme. To give a body to the three mirrors. To make it impossible to disappear into a crowd, forcing the minotaur to hide at best but never allowing him to forget the foreignness of himself, the unnatural space his body takes up. I think it's a standard feeling to want to be less invisible when one stands out against their will, but the beastly part of me tends to want to push against that feeling. Not only to keep standing out but to become so strange, to push it so far out of the ordinary that it negates the binary of visible and invisible and instead leads to deeper questions about myself and the world in which I exist, whether that world is the complete one or just the localized area of Dorsoduro. This is not sentimentality about madness or a suggestion that there is nobility in the suffering of being on the outside, but a personal philosophy that the true absurdness of the world is in its pretense that so much of life is not ridiculous. That the endless suffering, humiliation, grief, and pain caused by systems outside of one's control, circumstances already determined before one's birth, and the exhaustive process of having to create a good life for yourself and your family—a process that keeps one away from so much of what makes life worthwhile that at the end of it, what one feels is relief more than joy—all these things are natural parts of life, and a great sign of maturity, of being a true adult, is to simply accept them and keep striving, when the proper reaction should be instead to sit like Job and scream that none of it is deserved. That is what is ridiculous to me and what fascinates me about physical transformation. It is not absurd that someone would become a bird under great stress. What is absurd is that so many people do not.

The change into the minotaur happened after I heard the music of the man in black when I returned from San Marco. I was pulled over to the tunnel by the sound, but after arriving, I saw that there was no one there. I wondered whether I had imagined the music—that I was carrying it in my heart after that first time I had seen him. Without the man there, and still willing to risk missing some work, and perhaps not being ready to help my parents, I decided to exit the tunnel and walk about the basilica. But as soon as I stepped outside the tunnel and in front of the water under the small bridge, I felt lightheaded. A bout of vertigo, similar to how I used to feel when I dealt with intense cluster headaches and migraines, a trait I had inherited from my father and grandfather. With the pain came this feeling of a change of self; I was looking at the world from a much greater distance.

Looking at my reflection in the water, I saw the head of a bull, with a horn on each side, staring back at me. My body had also become larger, thicker, powerful but also cumbersome. I was heavy. My first reaction was a natural one—I thought I was dreaming. I tried to wake myself up the same way I had done sometimes with other nightmares. I closed my eyes and prayed, bargaining with God to let me be myself again, promising in return that I would try to be better than I had been before. I opened my eyes and saw the same bullheaded man and his dark eyes shining back at me. I closed them again, squinted, and prayed harder. I got on my knees by the water, praying like I used to at mass. I prayed to be me again. But I opened my eyes to the same eyes again. No matter how many times I tried to wake up to myself, all I saw was the minotaur's pathetic face. Panic set in.

If this was a dream, a nightmare, then it was one in which prayer would not help me escape. I thought of how I might reverse the transformation. My crime had been to go through the tunnel and back, and in my fear, I thought that if I could walk through it again, I could unbecome what I had become. I walked through and back. Nothing changed. I ran through and back. Nothing changed. I walked and ran through and walked back backward. Nothing changed. I ran back to the apartment, tears threatening to fall, and pushed my now giant shoulders through the small hallway and the first door to the left.

The apartment, which was already small before, felt miniscule in the new body. Inside, I cried. I cried the kind of tears that make the heart and shoulders shake. I cried until I cried out and heard the depth and terror of my new voice, which scared me into silence, both because I was now afraid of waking or alerting the people around me and because though I could see and feel the monster I was—I saw the reflection in the water and in the bathroom mirror—the inhuman cry underlined it in a way I couldn't deny.

For the next week, I didn't leave the apartment. I didn't eat or sleep. I was confined in my new body, so I confined myself away from the world. If I couldn't change myself back with prayer or by reversing the transformation, I could starve my body down until it disappeared. But after that week, nothing had changed. I was still as hulking as I was before, and now with the lack of sleep and food, I felt more and more like I was in a living nightmare.

Like any child in distress, I wanted my mother. I wanted to be cradled in her arms, to sit on her lap as she cracked my knuckles, wasting the hours talking about one Nigerian politician or another. Out of a fear of rejection, though, I never called her. It was better to be uncertain of her possible reaction than to call and have her tell me I was not the son she had before. For some reason, I believed my father would have accepted me immediately. In my imagination, he didn't reject me. Yet I also didn't call him either.

The person I called was Simon. He was the one who had said that it was a fantastical time in Venice, and it seemed he would be the most understanding about the fantastical actually happening. My instinct was correct. After I slowly explained to him what had happened, giving him as much information as possible and making sure he knew I was being serious rather than playing a strange joke—a joke that included a distinct change in the tone and tremor of my voice—he paused for what was probably a short time, though it seemed eternal to me, as I waited for his judgment. Then he asked if he could come over after his classes. He wanted to see the transformation in person.

He arrived in the evening. He had food and drinks. For the first hour, we talked as we usually did while he made tea and cooked in my small kitchen area. Then, after I ate and calmed down, when I was loosened up from the drinks, he began asking questions and examining me. He asked if he could touch me, and I let him. The feeling of his hands running across my neck, shoulders, and arms was strange in that it felt like I was an animal being inspected, and yet the feeling of being touched by another, by a friend, was something I didn't realize I had missed so much. He asked how it felt. I responded that being touched felt strange and complicated. But that wasn't the question he was asking.

He wanted to know how it felt to be what I was. To be a minotaur. To change into something else.

In my panic, and except for my initial feeling that the distance between me and the world had increased, I hadn't thought much about how it felt to be a minotaur. As a person, I wore masks and performed like everyone else, and with the change, it felt like a new level of performance had been added. I still felt like myself, just tilted slightly, and I now had to be the tilted me who was living in not only a new body but a body that didn't fit anywhere within the context of our world. Worst of all, I said to him, I didn't know how to go about this new role. I was lonely in a way I had never been before because I was now the only one of my kind. As a person, in my aloneness, I still knew there were billions of others who felt the same way. And as particular as that feeling was to their life, we were connected even with that separation, and I knew that whatever role I played had been played before by others. There were innumerable ways to be human, and I could pick and choose which paths fit my identity. In my loneliness as a minotaur, though, I was a complete exile, pushed completely outside of the world. There was no road for me.

The question I wanted answered was this: Why me? Why was I the one who changed, and why was this curse happening in a place that wasn't my home? There was no connection between me and Venice except that I found myself there at a strange time. But that didn't seem to be enough to justify what had happened. This wasn't how these kinds of transformations happened in the old stories. There wasn't anything grand or meaningful about me becoming a minotaur. More than anything, it felt as if it had happened by chance, as if I woke up one day to find myself in a different body and that was all there was to it. But certainly there were people who were more deserving of the punishment.

"Have you seen the winged lion at St. Mark's Square?" Simon asked. Yes, I had. "When you walk around Venice, you see many images of that winged lion everywhere, it's the symbol of the city. There's a story that before it was the winged lion, it had been a griffin. But the statue was repaired so often through the ages that it changed into what it is now. Now the world associates Venice with lions. We have them everywhere! From the basilicas to the Arsenale—lions, lions, lions!"

Then he took my heavy hand in his. "But how many real lions do you think have been in Venice?" I didn't know. "Exactly," he said. "Venice is the city of the winged lion, the former griffin, and real lions have rarely ever been here. It's a myth. This is the city of the fantastical. There's no reason why a minotaur couldn't also appear."

Before he left, Simon told me not to worry. He would try to find a way for me to exist in the city, at least until we figured out a longer-term solution or how to reverse the change. Two days passed without hearing from him, but both days, I heard knocks at the door, and, not seeing anyone through the peephole, I opened it to find food and drinks in plastic bags on the floor. The morning of the third day, Simon called and asked if he could bring some people to see me. They were politicians and other people with influence, people who he trusted and who could help us.

That night, in the cover of the darkness, Simon arrived outside the apartment and asked me to come outside. I hesitated. I trusted him, but I didn't feel safe. Not with the others. Yet I had no choice. I was in their city after all, and we needed a solution to my problem. I shifted out of the door and through the small hallway that squeezed my body, even as I tried to walk out facing the wall. I will never forget the faces of the six men when I emerged from the door. Simon had a satisfied look on his face. I imagined the men hadn't believed him when he told them about me, and he was enjoying being right, which is a thrill regardless of the circumstance. The men's expressions shifted from curiosity and concern to shock and fear as they looked up at the massive body towering over them.

No one spoke at first, and the silence made me uncomfortable. More than that, the size difference between me and them made me anxious. I knew I was large, but alone in my room, I was beginning to get used to it. Next to others, though, I realized how much bigger I was, and this difference terrified the men.

Soon they began inspecting me, but while Simon's examination had been done with care, I could see in their eyes and faces that below their curiosity were all the sinister thoughts of how I could be used for their own personal gain. Simon had reason to trust them, but men of that status don't get to their position without recognizing an opportunity to enrich themselves. I let them look at me and touch me. They asked no questions. Once they satisfied their eyes and hands, Simon asked me to go back inside. From the window of the living room, I heard them speaking as they left the area, but their conversation was in Italian, so all I could do was try to understand them through their tone of voice, which gave little away.

The next day, Simon arrived with a Black woman, an armed officer, and some news. When the officer and the woman saw me, they stepped back, and I saw a fear in their faces so genuine that it made me want to hide. Without thinking, I told them everything was fine as a way to alleviate their terror, which did little to make them more comfortable. It seemed to make matters worse, as they were then terrified that the beast could speak. Simon stopped their retreat by putting his hands on their backs, and he assured them I was harmless. He told me the woman was there to be my caretaker. She would do my shopping, cleaning, and anything else I needed. The armed man was my way to the outside world. Simon called him a guide, a protector, and I knew he was to be my chaperone. He would patrol the area during the day, and then when I wanted to go out for a late-night walk, he would go with me to inspect the area first and then guide me around. I was only mainly allowed to walk around the area of the Salute.

That's how it was for weeks. In the morning, the woman arrived to clean the apartment, and then at night, I walked around the Salute with the armed man following me. In between, Simon came to sit and drink tea with me and to give me any news.

When the woman cleaned, I tried to stay inside the bedroom so as not to scare her. Her fear didn't lessen, and when she came into the room to ask me what I wanted to eat, she tried her best to avoid looking at me, though her curiosity always got the better of her. She often peeked and then tried to immediately avoid my eyes. The armed man and I never spoke. After the initial shock from our first meeting, he took to his duties with the same discipline and routine of a standard assignment, which was both comfortable and harrowing.

The news Simon brought over the next few weeks was mostly about the conversations he had with the men he had brought with him that day—what they were thinking of doing with me. Some saw me as dangerous. They had debated cordoning off the area of Dorsoduro surrounding my apartment from the public while they figured out how to de-transform me or at least create a plan to send me away, but the plan was made difficult because it would arouse suspicion from the citizens who were finally able to enjoy the city by themselves. And of course, sneaking a minotaur onto an international flight was impossible.

They also considered the idea of using me as part of Venice's tourist attractions, to have the area around my apartment become the minotaur's lair, where visitors could come and take pictures of me. Like a mini amusement park, a smaller version of what many saw the city as. The pandemic had hit the city hard, and with the loss of revenue from tourists, anything that could bring in more visitors and money once the world returned to normal would be welcome. With the advances in technology and special effects, they could sell me as a fiction, and all I would have to do is play the role of the minotaur. It was a role I was still figuring out, but I imagined what they wanted was for me to walk around scaring people and growling at them while making while making myself visible for photos, like a mascot at Disney World.

They also suggested that I be killed. In order to avoid the trouble of figuring out how I was to exist, and trouble with the city's citizens—and its tourists when the world opened up again—the best and simplest solution was to get rid of me. They didn't want to rile people up at a sensitive time, in either direction. The logic was understandable. But I didn't want to die. I was a monster, I looked and felt like one, and at the time I couldn't imagine what kind of life I would lead in the world, but I didn't want to die. I still loved life. My existence was as miraculous as it always had been.

There were some other suggestions that I be put in San Giorgio Maggiore or one of the basilicas, where the men and women of the church could look after me and I could contribute by managing the building at night.

Simon told me to relax, that there were still a lot of conversations to be had and that he would make sure that, at the least, I stayed alive. This was a small consolation to me as I started realizing the possibility that I could die in my new body. It didn't occur to me until then that the transformation could be permanent. That I would never again see the day and the night like the old me again.

I was despairing over this thought so much that I waved away the cleaning woman's requests to shop for food and drinks. I didn't want anything; I was starving myself again. She always finished her tasks quickly, and when she walked out of the building, I would go back to the living room to have more space for my sadness. One day I overheard her talking to someone on her phone while cleaning. Normally, she and I spoke English to each other, and when she spoke to Simon, she used Italian. But that day, she spoke in a language that caught my ear from recognition. It had a familiarity and warmth that English didn't have for me, and the sound of it made me happy until what she said became clear to me. Her words floated fatally through the dark night like poisonous fog as she told someone on the other side of the call, in Igbo, that she was being forced to clean for a demon. The word she used, in translation, was closer to "devil." The other person must have not believed her, and so as she disappeared further into the city, I heard her protesting that I was in fact a demon, a devil in flesh and blood.

After that, I resigned myself to my fate. I was to die a minotaur and to live alone, unable to walk to the places I enjoyed in the city—to have lunch outside at restaurants again, to look at and buy pastries, to buy prosecco and vanilla wafers, to visit Orient Experience II to buy the same rice and beef meal on my own, to be extended the normal care that one person gives to another on the simple basis that they both recognize the other's humanity. All of that was gone.

Later that night, I found out my presence had been discovered by more people outside of the small group that had seen me. After I readied myself to go for my routine walk, I heard the armed man talking to some young kids—four teenagers led by a blond boy who had the build and physical grace of a footballer. He carried himself lightly through the world, as if he was floating even when he was standing still. The armed man was warning them off, but the kids must have heard a rumor that there was something strange in the building, and the presence of the armed man confirmed it enough that they weren't easily dissuaded. I decided to stay inside that night.

The next day, Simon called me to talk about the teenagers. The armed man had reported it to him. The others were panicking. The teenagers were evidence that the news had slipped out. Soon everyone else would know that there was something unusual going on, and more people would come investigate. Simon told me to stay inside until they figured something out. The small freedom I had was gone.

I stayed inside the apartment for the full day after that, which transitioned to night and then day and then night without anything of note happening. The arrival and departure of the cleaning woman was so routine that it only added to the sameness of my imprisonment. That's what it was. I was imprisoned in my apartment in that area of Venice. I was imprisoned in the body of the minotaur.

Eventually, I rebelled. I had to see the world, or at least my little slice of it. So in between the time when the cleaner left and the armed man arrived, I began going out on my own. I hid at the furthest point of the Salute, and then when it was dark enough, when I was sure there was no one in the streets, I walked counterclockwise to the other side to avoid being seen by the armed man. All I did in my freedom was visit the places I had visited in my human form. I went to the grocery store. I walked by the water around the Zattere stop. I went to Santa Margherita, taking in the restaurants and bars there as if it was the first time I had seen them. Which in a way was true—it was the first time I was seeing the area as a minotaur. I saw the orange light that meant that Orient Experience II was open, and getting closer but still remaining out of sight, I saw that the Black waiter was still there working. I wanted more than anything to walk in and have the same small talk we always did, to connect through the small bridge of conversation, but I knew that would expose me to more people. And worst of all, if he saw me and rejected me, it would have pushed me into further despair. I didn't need to bridge the gap between me and the world that I used to know; it was good enough for me to simply know the world and its people outside of my prison still existed. To be able to see that world with my eyes.

I was on my way back, lost in thought and forgetting myself, in that narrow path before the corner pub, when I heard the sound of footsteps and the voices of teenagers coming from the other side. I was a bit past where I had bought pizza for the first time when they saw me. It seemed they were coming back from visiting the apartment again because they reacted with glee at their curiosity being confirmed. The leader had a weapon in his hand; it looked like a hammer in the dark. I remember thinking about how large and menacing the instrument looked in the hand of a child. They ran toward me. I couldn't turn to run backward. I was too big. I was trapped.

Before I knew it, they had me on the ground sideways. At that moment, I was scared. I was scared like a human, so much like a child, that I forgot the new body I was in and its physical power. The others held me down, and their leader hit my right horn with his hammer. Over and over, he smashed the weapon on the horn. I wanted to scream, but though the pain was mine and brought tears to my eyes, I felt I was watching them mutilate me from afar. I groaned, but I didn't scream. I don't know how long the beating lasted, but when they were done, they ran away with my bloodied horn, their prize.

I returned to the apartment. I told the armed man what had happened. He alerted Simon, who showed up thirty minutes later. While listening to my explanation, soothing my pains and chiding me for going out on my own, he also helped me move my belongings to the Salute. The apartment wasn't safe anymore. With the move, I could hide again. There would be no guard to make sure there was no indication of where

I was. It was sure that the kids would tell more people, and those people would come looking for their piece of the beast.

I moved from Calle Lanza to a room inside the church. There, I fell into a deeper depression. With it being December, solidly winter, no visitors came in anymore. Even the priest was nowhere to be found. No more mass. Just me and the paintings most of the time. The cleaning woman still came by with food and drinks and to tend to my wound. She went about her job the same as always, not knowing that I knew what she thought of me.

For three days, this was the routine of my life. But where the imprisonment before had made me want to venture outside, this time, with the loss of my horn and the shame of the defeat—which was a violent confirmation that I was not human—I wanted to be out of the city and my body completely.

Without anyone guarding the door, I went outside to the water bus stop. I looked at my reflection in the water, ugly and broken. I wanted that look to be the last one. I was determined to drown in the dark mirror of the water, when I heard the voices of the teenagers again. They had gone back looking for me. I turned to run back into the basilica in case they came in my direction. But at the top of the stairs, I stopped. I was ashamed of my own cowardice. I asked myself what I was running for. Fear turned to anger.

They should be the ones afraid of me. And anger became the foundation for revenge. At the top of the stairs, I didn't forget myself. I knew and accepted what I was. The kids had reminded me of that, and my missing horn was evidence enough. I was the beast.

I went to my enemies. When they saw me again, there was the same glee in their eyes. A glee of stupidity, the naivety of children who were too slow to read the changed dynamic of the situation. I charged toward them, and then they were the ones who were scared. They screamed and ran. The leader with his hammer was the last one to flee. But I was much faster. He only took a few steps before I was upon him. I rushed and knocked him over, bouncing him off the wall. His friends disappeared around the corner. They abandoned him. Weak and bloodied, he turned over on his back, and in his fear, I saw him for what he was. A child. A powerless child. He begged in Italian, and without understanding the language, I knew he was begging me not to kill him.

But then all of it was over. I was again standing inside the tunnel before the bridge to the Salute after the man in black had finished his playing and disappeared into the night. Perhaps I had changed back. Perhaps I had never changed at all. But now I was me. My phone vibrated with emails and messages from work, and I saw a text from my mother with the singular "help," which I knew meant something had gone wrong with Microsoft Teams. Knowing that she was close to panicking, I hurried back to the apartment to see how I could fix the problem before getting ready for the meetings I had that night.

13

There were two things Simon especially wanted me to experience while I was in Venice. One was the high tide—the seasonal flooding. In 2019, the city had dealt with the second-highest tide ever recorded, which submerged St. Mark's Square under more than a meter of water. In October of 2020, a month before I arrived, a project known as MOSE went into operation. The project is a multibillion-dollar flood barrier and dam system that was started in 1984 and had been plagued by corruption, delays, and cost overruns. 2020 was finally to be the year to see whether the wait and the price for the barrier was worth it.

The second event was the Feast of the Madonna della Salute. This took place on November 21, which was the day in 1687 when the basilica next door to my apartment was completed, honoring a vow the doge had made to build a temple of great majesty for the Madonna for saving Venice from the plague. On that day every year, there is a great procession of Venetians from all over the city who make their way to the basilica to pay their respects, light a candle, and pray for good health.

The high tide was supposed to arrive a day after the feast. On the morning of November 21, I left the apartment, ready to walk as usual. I was so used to my routine that I forgot the day and its significance until I went out of the building and looked ahead to the end of Calle Lanza, at the intersection where C. Barbaro becomes C. S. Gregorio. I saw people streaming by. Young and old couples, families, old men by themselves, and young women with their groups of friends. They kept going and went without seeing me. I felt like a specter observing the residents of a different world. I didn't join the crowd. I could have gone to the church alone and lit candles with everyone or when no one was around, but I didn't think it was right for me to participate in a ceremony that was not for me.

I stayed away from the basilica until the evening. People were still going to the church, but these were the stragglers who couldn't make it in the morning. I went back to the apartment, but rather than resting, I was pulled by curiosity toward the church. The festival was not for me, but it would have been a great missed opportunity to not witness the event. When I went, I saw tens of people holding candles and saying their prayers. Because of the pandemic, the ceremony had been held outside, and I stood some distance away from the others.

The high tide didn't come the next day. The projection of rain was less than the disaster of 2019, but the MOSE project worked. Activated overnight, it shielded the city from the high waters, allowing Venetians to skip their annual exercise of dealing with the flooding. When Simon and I met for lunch a few days afterward, I mentioned how the high tide never came. He had been out of town. He said that he was disappointed I didn't get to see one of the city's traditions, but he said I had still gotten to witness a miracle—that the MOSE project had been launched after all the corruption.

14

There are about 390 bridges in Venice. They are inconsequential at the singular level, but added together, they hold collective power, pulling the city splintered by water together. I had my favorites during my time there. One of them was the bridge right after the Guggenheim Museum. If I was to name it, I would call it the Bridge of Deep Breaths. It was there that I always took a few minutes to rest and collect myself after a day of walking around. Before I turned in for the night, I would look out from that small window at the water and at the small boats passing by.

One afternoon, I drank a lot at the bar in Santa Margherita and was trying to hurry home to recover a bit before work. Even in a hurry, I arrived at the bridge and couldn't help but spend some minutes leaning over it, and as usual, when I'm a bit drunk, a strong feeling of sadness and aloneness came over me.

Since childhood, water has had a great effect on me. When I was young, my mother's family tried to teach my older brother and me how to swim. Children from her village learned to swim very early, but we grew up mostly in my father's village, around more farms than water. My grandmother tried to teach us in the way she taught the other children, which meant she took us to the water and set us free; we were to figure it out with some encouragement.

As my mother describes it, my father immediately ran into the water and pulled the two of us out. He lambasted my mother and her mother. The two women laughed at him, and my grandmother told him that we wouldn't be able to learn anything if he didn't let us struggle.

I love the water. Rivers, lakes, seas, and oceans. When I think of the best life for myself, it is next to the water. Other circumstances of that life can change, but what doesn't change is the water. I need to be near it and feel it close to me.

On the bridge with my eyes closed, I saw myself floating on the waters of the lagoon. Floating and drifting away on top of the water, that was peace. Being carried away, facing the moon and the stars—that's how I always saw myself in the world, with the aloneness, distance, and lightness of that feeling. A necessary lightness to counter the heaviness underneath the surface, the destructive power of the world the water represented. The surface of the water also suggests the possibility of being taken under, and this potential for drowning has its pull as well.

Once, on a weekend trip in college, my friends and I went to one of the lakes around Detroit. As a game, some of the boys decided to race to a buoy in the distance and then come back. To swim faster, I went underwater. When I told this story years later, I said that beneath the surface of the water, I lost one of my contacts and, in trying to rub the stinging out of my eyes, I sank. But that's not totally honest.

What happened was that deep inside the water, I lost the lightness. I forgot myself. I stopped swimming and looked in awe at the dark blue of the water, with its pressures all around me. I was overwhelmed and heartbroken, though I didn't know why the view pained me so much. It seemed to happen in an instant, but when I came to my senses, I realized I had been sinking the whole time. My body went into shock. It panicked and thrashed, trying to get us back to the surface. I watched myself struggling from outside myself. I remember the exact thought that came to me as my exhausted body tried and failed to surface, falling back deeper into the water. Looking at the light reflecting off the top of the water, I thought, "This isn't a bad way to go." Luckily, a lifeguard came to my rescue.

While reminiscing about this near-death incident, I drifted off to sleep on the Bridge of Deep Breaths. A few minutes later, I was awakened by the sound of heels hitting the street. Tired and tipsy, I made my way back to the apartment.

There are a few more bridges I developed an affinity for while I was in Venice. There's the most famous one, the Bridge of Sighs, which Ethan showed me after we walked through Piazza San Marco. The bridge was built in 1600 to connect the New Prison to the interrogation rooms in the doge's palace. The legend is that before being imprisoned, convicts would look out from the bridge and sigh at the view, savoring it in the knowledge that they wouldn't see it for a long time. Like all legends, there's uncertainty whether this is true or not. The bridge is considered one of the most romantic spots in Venice; many couples kiss under it while riding in gondolas, and Lord Byron famously references it in *Childe Harold's Pilgrimage*. In normal times, we would have been able to walk across the bridge and take photos—just like the countless other photos that have been taken from the bridge—but I liked that we weren't able to. Regardless of whether the myth of the bridge was true or not, I felt uncomfortable about seeing such an object as romantic, considering that its function was to transport people from one state of being, of existing in the world, to another, of being disappeared.

There is also the bridge after Taverna San Trovaso. On that bridge one day, I nodded and said "Ciao" to a Black woman and her son, who were walking the opposite way as me. She had the child by hand and responded with a smile and "Ciao, bello," the first time I heard the phrase. I looked it up, and seeing the meaning, stood on the bridge, smiling at my phone.

Another bridge became significant to me because of an encounter I had with someone else on it. It happened on the day when I decided to finally enter the pastry shop near Piazzale Roma. The bridge goes across the Rio del Malpaga canal from Fondamenta Toletta, but it is not the bridge that goes ahead to Ponte de la Toletta but the one at the intersection of Fondamenta Lombardo and Fondamenta Borgo—right after the Agenzia Nautica Base. It's such an ordinarily inconsequential bridge, except on that day when I crossed it along with a handful of other people. When I looked up on the bridge, I saw a Black man to my left asking passersby for change. I couldn't hear him over the music in my headphones, but when our eyes met, he beckoned me over. I turned my eyes away and walked past him.

Shame stopped me in front of Santa Maria dei Carmini. I knew what had made me avert my eyes, to look away from someone who had only wanted for us to recognize each other in a foreign world. He was looking to me as I had looked at the waiter in Orient Experience II. The waiter welcomed my recognition—I turned away from the other man. It's easier to validate connection when the other person is seen as worthwhile. I had shifted my eyes away from the other man because I didn't want those around us to see the two of us as being connected. He was begging for money. There was a great distance between us, and I wanted that acknowledged. A shame—by turning from him, I told the man and myself that we were not alike.

Maybe the statement is true—true connection and solidarity need more than color to mean anything. But it is also a bridge. I stopped in Santa Maria dei Carmini, and

though a dark part of me wanted to keep walking, I turned
toward Santa Margherita to find an ATM. I took out twenty
euros and then walked back to the bridge where the man
was. On the way back, I had a sinking feeling I wouldn't see
the man again, and so I wouldn't have the chance to atone for
my cowardice. I imagined returning to find the man gone, of
being left out on the bridge with the money and knowledge
that when someone reached out to me, I had rejected them.

He was still there when I went back, staring out from
the bridge. I gave him the money, and he thanked me in
Italian. I gestured that I didn't speak Italian, but that was
no problem—he knew English well enough to carry on
a conversation. I didn't ask if he knew English from the
necessity of having to encounter English-speaking tourists
in Venice or if he had learned it as a way to survive in
his journeys, but once he found out I was Nigerian, his
face lit up. He was Nigerian as well. He was actually from
Anambra state, where my mother is from. I joked to him
that I could be anywhere in the world and somehow I
would run into a Nigerian, and on that small bridge, we
exchanged stories about our lives up until that point. He
had arrived in Venice a few years earlier after making his
way through other parts of Italy. He asked me about the
United States, New York City in particular, and at the end,
he told me to greet my mother for him, as if they knew one

another. A few times after that, I would be walking around lost in thought, and then I'd hear him yell "Brother!" in the specific way Nigerians sound that word.

15

My initial sense of Venice as a big labyrinth was confirmed through walks, the books that I read, and the feelings I had being there at a time, as Simon had said, that was fantastical. Each time I stepped out of my apartment building or turned a corner, there was a sense, a thrill and fear of possibility, that I would enter into something, somewhere, completely different. I felt it most readily in familiar streets, which may sound contradictory, though it's not. Transformation, for me, has to come through the familiar, through the ordinary. It was only because I began to know the streets so well that they could catch me by surprise.

In the ordinary, one's guard is down. By making a routine of my days, I made the experience of Venice banal. In order to be comfortable there, I had to make the city known to me. I had to make it a kind of home, and no matter where a home is—in Venice, New York, Paris, London, Lagos, Dakar—it becomes normal and standard once you've gone to the grocery store enough times. One eventually knows a home so well that the fantasy of it gets replaced by the material reality. It's a reality that has its own magic, but after so much time, one comes to know what is possible and what is not. A routine is a routine because there's control to it.

By creating a routine in the small part of Dorsoduro that I haunted, I made Venice graspable. But it was in those moments when I wasn't consciously thinking of it as a site for the surreal that the possibility of it turning surreal was at its highest. When frustrated by work or my parents' constant asking for help with one thing or another, or angry at feeling someone's eyes on me, when I stormed through the streets, when my guard was completely down—that's when the fantastical had to happen.

Magic can also be created. All it takes is adding some uncertainty to the routine of everyday life. To break the daze in which many of us go from one day to the next. In Venice, it could have been as simple as taking the opposite path around the Salute, going to Africa Experience rather than Orient Experience, or leaving my phone at home and going deeper into the fear of being lost.

On a day I didn't have my phone with me, I decided to follow the dogs of Venice. I was fascinated by them because they were so well-behaved. They didn't bark, and without being on leashes, they followed their owners obediently while exploring the world around them on their own.

There was one owner and his dog that I followed after taking a left by the grocery store, heading toward the Zattere stop. Instead of going toward Ponte Longo, a path

I was familiar with, the two of them headed the opposite direction, toward Ponte dei Incurabili.

What amused me on the walk were the numerous times the dog would turn down a side street, sniffing something only it could sense. As it did so, the owner kept walking without so much as glancing back. He was the Venetian Lot. After going off to explore whatever caught its attention, the dog would perk its head up as if calculating its owner's location, and then it would scramble around the streets until it had returned to Lot's side.

When I finally decided to break from the two of them, I looked around and had no idea where I was. Rather than being anxious at being lost, I was so inspired by the dog that I decided to walk around following whatever caught my interest, assuming that I would eventually find my way back to the apartment or at least somewhere familiar enough. In the worst-case scenario, I could head toward the water and take a bus back to a familiar stop. For the rest of the day, I explored, turning down roads based only on feeling.

When I returned to the apartment, I messaged Ted about seeing Venice as a labyrinth and about the idea that the surreal could only break through in an ordinary moment. I kept the following of the dog to myself. In response, he suggested I visit San Giorgio Maggiore—there was apparently something there that was perfect for me and what I was thinking about.

The next morning, I boarded the water bus. The ride was about twenty minutes, and as usual, I was one of only a handful of people on the boat. By the time we reached San Giorgio, I was the last passenger left.

Almost everything on the island was closed, though the Vatican chapels, Cini Foundation, and the Basilica di San Giorgio Maggiore were still spectacular from the outside. Walking clockwise around the basilica, I saw a great line of white boats like a gathering of seagulls at the yacht harbor.

I thought I was alone on the island until I walked past the lone café, which faced out to the harbor. The door was open, though from the outside, I didn't see anyone initially. I wasn't hungry, and though I usually like sitting in empty restaurants and bars, something kept me outside of that one. I walked all the way to the small pier on the far right, which had areas where one could sit and watch the water and the boats going by. Then I walked past the café again, trying to figure out what I was supposed to be seeing. That's when I saw the bartender inside. He was cleaning glasses and looking up at a football match on the TV to his left. I must have watched him for some time because he felt my eyes on him, looked forward, and smiled. I made a weak attempt at a wave.

Between the café and the Le Stanze del Vetro museum next to it was a path that went into the island, which I had disregarded because the museum was closed. But it was actually the road to what I was there to see. Unlike the other parts of the island, the road was made of rocks and gravel. To my delight and surprise, right behind the café was an incredible garden, a labyrinth-garden inspired by "The Garden of Forking Paths" by Borges.

The story of the labyrinth in San Giorgio Maggiore was that it was dreamt up by Randoll Coate, an English diplomat and maze architect, who had been introduced to Borges in the 1950s. Coate dreamt that he and his friend agreed to build something to honor the writer. Because it was Borges, the monument had to be a labyrinth. Coate wrote about his plans to Susana Bombal, and after her death, the letter was discovered by her nephew, Camilo Aldao, who then went to meet the architect to talk about building the structure. A story of creation worthy enough to be included in any book of Borges's fictions.

The labyrinth's first iteration was created in 2003, in the province of Mendoza in Argentina. The Venetian one was inaugurated in June of 2011, on the twenty-fifth anniversary of Borges's death. It was built through a collaboration between Fondazione Cini and the Jorge Luis Borges International Foundation, and it remained faithful to Coate's original design. It is one of the three cloisters on the island—along with the Palladian Cloister and the Cypress Cloister—and they were all fenced off and locked during the time I was there.

The garden contained more than three thousand buxus sempervirens bushes, each over thirty-five inches tall, and the design of the labyrinth, seen from above, was that of a book. Inside the garden are references to Borges, including his name duplicated and mirrored, hourglasses, his walking stick, his age at his death, a question mark, the sign of infinity, and the initials of his widow, Maria Kodama, who led the inauguration of the garden in Venice. She was also instrumental in building the one in Argentina.

When I approached the entrance, the gate was locked. In normal times, guided tours are given through the labyrinth, which is wonderfully ironic. But in abnormal times, there was no way in. I walked back and forth, trying to find another possible way into the garden. I wanted to walk around inside it, to see everything for myself—the hourglass, the mirrored names, the infinity sign, and the walking stick. But there was no opening.

Well, there was an easy way to get in. The fence around the garden was low, low enough that I could have easily hopped it. I had hopped much taller fences before. As I tried to find another entrance, I kept thinking, "Just hop the fence." But as soon as I grabbed onto it and readied myself, I heard footsteps on the gravel. I looked back and saw three young people, two girls and one guy. They had turned down the path and were walking toward me. I pulled back and ran my hand along the gate, pretending to admire its craftsmanship. The three of them didn't stay long. They didn't seem that interested in the garden or the other cloisters. They smiled at me, walked around, pulled at the gates that were locked, and, disappointed, went back toward the harbor.

Their appearance made me reconsider jumping the gate completely. The consequences of getting caught weren't worth it, especially since I already stood out. The shame of being caught and possibly arrested while being one of the few Black people around at the time would have been too much to endure.

By the time I came back out to the pier, the three other visitors were gone. The island belonged to me and the man at the café again. I spent the next few hours sitting by the water, reading on my phone, and looking out to the water every few minutes. A few boats went by, and some of their operators smiled and waved at me.

16

A few days into December, I wanted to go home. The situation with the virus was getting exponentially worse again, and I wanted to be with my parents through whatever was to come. I had to protect them, and the thought followed me around everywhere I went in Venice. Ted and I arranged for me to leave on the seventh.

Until that day of departure arrived, I did what I always did. I went on my daily walks that ended in the evenings when I had to work and help my parents. I went to Orient Experience II, the basilica, and even journeyed out to San Marco to look at the high-end boutique stores and buy some wine.

When I told my parents I was coming home soon, they were both overjoyed, and my father, who had never before been expressive about love, was suddenly and surprisingly open about wanting to have me at home.

Now here, I want to defend my father. Not from his enemies, or from the humiliations of the world which he has carried so willingly through his life, but from myself, my younger self, who in his desire for self-determination couldn't see what was going on beyond his immediate struggle.

Speaking now, from the distance afforded by transformation, by time, by the alleviation of poverty, now that the walls don't feel like they're closing in every waking second—speaking from that place of reflection, I can say that I wish I had been different. It's a pointless statement but one I still want to make. It is pointless because I know if I were placed in the same situation again, even with this knowledge I have now, I would still behave the same way.

But I make this statement with sympathy and regret. By luck, my father was presented with a terrible choice—to stay in Nigeria with all of its comforts, with his dreams and his people, or to sell his inheritance and leave his siblings, nieces, nephews, cousins, friends, students, his identity, all for the sake of possibly providing a better life for his children. He made the choice he made and dealt with the consequences, in his body and in his mind.

Over the last few years, my father would sometimes ask my mother or me to help him with his eye drops. A doctor prescribed them to help lessen the pressure in my father's right eye, which had swelled from high levels of stress. Most of the time he could do it on his own, but because his hands shake when doing simple tasks, he could also miss his target. And he disliked wasting the drops. When squeezing the eye drops for my father, I often felt embarrassed of myself. This problem with his eye, along with the problems with his hands and his back, his depression, and his sadness, were the price he paid for our lives. The least I could have done for him was be kinder. To have seen the world beyond my own pain.

In the years that my father and I fought all the time, and I was punished so much that it isolated me from him and my siblings, my mother was the only person I confided in. She knew and saw everything that was happening, and she stepped in to protect me as much as she could. So many times, she warned me not to hold the anger too deeply—to bear it more lightly as a responsibility to myself and my father, "your son."

She wasn't asking me to forgive him, but she was saying I should recognize I was, in a way, stronger than he was. The world touched him in a way that it didn't touch me, and she knew that one day, our conditions would change, and she was urging me not to create too much distance before then. My mother was right. Yes, I wish in those days I could have endured the hatred more lightly, but more than that, I wish I could have given my father what he needed at that time. A simple thing that he asked for: a well-behaved son. Someone who played the role of the good child, went to class, got the best grades, graduated, and then found a good and stable job. I wish I could have gritted my teeth and done the things that made me unhappy, curbed my own need for self-determination, my own rage and frustration, at least for a few years, so that he didn't have to leave his school weekly to come and get me. So that he didn't have to come home angry all the time, on top of the other humiliations he suffered outside. If I had been a little bit better, life would have been easier for him.

But I wasn't. Rather than facing the world together, as father and son, we were enemies. When he should have taken me into his arms, he struck me. And when I should have given him grace, I shut myself away from him. I told him no. So many times I told him no. And we lost many years because of it.

One night, after I had left college, I was opening the front door of the house to drive to downtown Detroit when he stopped me. He asked where I was going. I reacted angrily, telling him I was simply going out. My anger didn't catch him by surprise, but it hurt him, and he said, in a low voice, almost to himself, that he didn't know why I hated him so much.

I remember looking at him with such anger at that moment. Everything he did to me, he seemed to have forgotten. The lines that the belt left on my skin meant nothing to him. Every single day that I hated being in that house because he made it impossible for me to come out of my room without being demeaned—it was all a distant memory for him. All the years I walked around silent and with my head down to avoid catching anyone's eyes because I was the bad one and no one wanted to be near the bad one because they had watched me be punished in front of them, had watched me be accused of so many things. Some of those things I was guilty of, and some I wasn't, but none of that mattered because I was the bad one. I hated him because he hated me first. Because he showed me how to hate someone.

He didn't understand it anymore because I was the victor. I had outlasted him. At the end of it, I was the one who had my life. I was the healthy one, the one who traveled, the one who looked after himself. I didn't need him. I will never forget bleeding on the ground after being stabbed and I did not think of it. That's how far he was from me back then. I had fought for myself, and I had won. Yet standing at the door, nothing about the victory felt good. The price of it had been too heavy—the loss of years, the distance between us. He was scared of me. He would rather ask my mother to call and see how I was doing than reach out on his own. I didn't recognize it for a long time, but our positions had switched.

No more. That's what I said to myself that day. No more of the hate. What was done was done. Some distance would always remain between us, but much of it could be closed. What my freedom gave me the opportunity to do was to be of service to him, and to be of service to my mother and siblings. Starting from zero, I had shaped my life into what I wanted it to be, and after seeing all the different kinds of my selves in the world, after leaving all the time only to return, the irony was that I wanted to be in the same position where they had started me, helping them through their days. The same child in the classroom with them, the same child in the ice cream truck with my father.

17

One night, after I had become a man again, Simon and I had dinner together. I was still overjoyed by my renewed personhood, at being back within the story of humanity—still an other but an other within the story. Simon asked me whether the minotaur killed the boy. At first I said no—both of them only needed to know he was capable of doing so. But maybe he did, maybe he crossed that line, so that when he became me again, there would always be the taste, the memory, the crime that forever marked what I had been before.

But that night, most of our conversation was about our happiness at the curse being lifted. Before Simon left, he told me that maybe I shouldn't think of the transformation as a curse so much—that there are some people who wish they could transform into a beast or a tree to express the deep pain they hold in all the time. "What you have been blessed with," Simon said, "is contact with another world beyond us. That shouldn't be taken completely as a negative."

On my last evening in Venice, I stopped by the shop of a glassblower close to my apartment. He was in there working on his craft alone. I stood outside for about ten minutes, watching him work. Usually after I watched him, I went back to the apartment, but since it was my last night, I decided to finally go in. The man was short and heavy, and he had very hard and worn hands. He looked ancient, not in outward age but in the graceful way he moved himself. He seemed like an extension of the city itself, as beautiful and grand as the basilica.

I asked him to make me two necklaces. One for me and one for my youngest brother. His name was Giorgio and he offered me a seat, and for the next hour, we talked about what was happening with the world, the lack of tourists, his family's long lineage with glassblowing, and the kind of Europeans and Americans who were the most annoying. Next to my seat was a stack of notebooks. I asked if I could look through them, and he said yes. They were a collection of notes about glassblowing in Italian, and though I couldn't read them, I enjoyed flipping through them.

As Giorgio the glassblower made two circular necklaces for me—one red and one black—I thought how he was a man who you could sit opposite for an hour as he worked as if you weren't there. Someone who was so deeply part of Venice that he went on the same way whether people were around or not. A minotaur's friend.

After an hour, Giorgio put the two necklaces on silver chains and wrapped them up for me. I promised him I would visit him again the next time I was in Venice. That night, I barely did any work. A boat was arranged to take me to the airport early in the morning. When I woke up, I saw a strange number had texted me with directions on where to meet for the ride. When I arrived, there was a man there who was extraordinarily friendly for that time of day. He helped me onto the boat, and in the cover of the darkness that winter morning, we raced to the small Marco Polo Airport.

Acknowledgements

Thank you to everyone who made this book possible, including:

Ted Philipakos, for all of his help, guidance, and accommodation that made any of this possible.

Simon Levis Sullam, for walking me around the city of Venice and being a wonderful friend and educator during that time.

Ben Carrington, for the whiskey, friendship, and generosity.

Zoé Samudzi, for suffering all the different versions of this book that I sent her during its writing.

David Myers, for his friendship, knowledge, and ability to connect people around the world.

Nomi Stolzenberg, for her friendship, intelligence, and sensitivity to my writing.

Ty Stiklorius, for being an incredible person and supporter, as well as being a truly kind and generous person.

Anne Trubek, for believing in the book to begin with and the confidence that it should be as weird and particular as it should be.

Phoebe Mogharei, for all of her work getting the book to people and believing in its quality.

Michael Jauchen, for his careful editing and patience with my late emails.

David Wilson, for a wonderfully designed cover.

Zack Goldman and Eric Beard, who have greatly helped me for the last ten years.

Supriya Nair, for her fantastic sense of taste and her support of my writing from the beginning.

Ladan Osman, who understood the minotaur before anyone else.

Michelle Kuo, who I could spend days with walking through Paris and talking about books.

Linda Brindeau, a patient friend and even more patient French teacher.

Veery Huleatt, who has suffered through my endless ramblings on everything surreal and literary.

My father, mother, and siblings. And my grandparents on both sides.

All of my friends in Venice, who I spent the fantastical time with eating pizza, walking around, and talking about labyrinths and mirrors.

And Giorgio Nason, the glassblower who made the necklace that I still wear today, and who instantly recognized me when I returned years later.

About the Author

Zito Madu is a Nigerian-born writer who grew up in Detroit, Michigan. He's been a narrative director at several creative agencies, a sportswriter, a soccer player, and an engineering student. His writing has been appeared in *Plough Quarterly*, *Victory Journal*, *GQ Magazine*, the *New Republic*, and the *Nation*. He lives in Brooklyn.